The Sneaky Book for Girls

THE SNEAKY BOOK FOR GIRLS

How to perform sneaky magic tricks, escape a grasp, use sneaky codes and ciphers, detect counterfeit currency, and make spy devices, backpacks, and sneaky accessories

Cy Tymony

Andrews McMeel
Publishing, LLC
Kansas City

08 09 10 11 12 MLT 10 9 8 7 6 5 4 3 2 1

ISBN-13: 978-0-7407-7714-1
ISBN-10: 0-7407-7714-9

Library of Congress Control Number: 2008926294

www.andrewsmcmeel.com

Disclaimer

This book is for the entertainment and edification of its readers. While reasonable care has been exercised with respect to its accuracy, the publisher and the author assume no responsibility for errors or omissions in its content. Nor do we assume liability for any damages resulting from use of the information presented here.

This book contains references to electrical safety that *must* be observed. *Do not use AC power for any projects listed.* Do not place or store magnets near such magnetically sensitive media as video-tapes, audiotapes, or computer disks.

Disparities in materials and design methods and the application of the components may cause results to vary from those shown here. The publisher and the author disclaim any liability for injury that may result from the use, proper or improper, of the information contained in this book. We do not guarantee that the information contained herein is complete, safe, or accurate, nor should it be considered a substitute for your good judgment and common sense.

Nothing in this book should be construed or interpreted to infringe on the rights of other persons or to violate criminal statutes. We urge you to obey all laws and respect all rights, including property rights, of others.

Contents

Danger Girl

Crafty Girl

Magic Girl

Acknowledgments

I'd like to thank my agents, Sheree Bykofsky and Janet Rosen, for believing in my *Sneaky Uses* book concept from the start. A very special thanks goes to Katie Anderson, my editor at Andrews McMeel, for her invaluable direction and support on this project.

I'm grateful to the following people who assisted me in spreading the word about the *Sneaky* books: Ira Flatow, Gayle Anderson, Sandy Cohen, Katey Schwartz, Cherie Courtade, Susan Casey, Mike Suan, John Schatzel, Mark Frauenfelder, Melissa Gwynne, Steve Cochran, Christopher G. Selfridge, Timothy M. Blangger, Charles Bergquist, Phillip M. Torrone, Paul and Zan Dubin Scott, Dana Vinke, Cynthia Hansen, Charles Powell, Harmonie Tangonan, and Bruce Pasarow.

I'm thankful for project evaluation and testing assistance provided by Sybil Smith, Isaac English, and Bill Melzer.

And a special thanks to Helen Cooper, Clyde Tymony, George and Zola Wright, Ronald Mitchell, and to my mother, Cloise Shaw, for providing me with positive motivation and support for an early foundation in science, and a love of reading.

Introduction

Girls like to know something that others do not and to fool their friends with magic tricks and illusions. Yet, many girls do not receive guidance and a science education that relates to the real world, and this explains why they may not excel in science and technology later in life. *The Sneaky Book for Girls* provides a way to learn the basic principles of science and have fun at the same time.

The Sneaky Book for Girls shows you how to use everyday items to adapt unique gadgets, secure personal items, and get the upper hand on aggressors. Girls will learn how to be real-life improvisers in minutes, using nothing but a few hodgepodge items fate has put at their disposal. *The Sneaky Book for Girls* is packed with science projects, sneaky product-reuse applications, and magic tricks for girls to challenge at a moment's notice with just paper and cardboard while demonstrating how to conserve our resources.

For lovers of sneaky tricks, personal protection techniques, and gadgetry, *The Sneaky Book for Girls* is a unique assortment of over forty fabulous build-it-yourself projects, self-defense and survival strategies, and fun magic tricks. *The Sneaky Book for Girls* also highlights amazing stories about remarkable women inventors, scientists, and even spies, which will amaze and inspire. After finishing the book, girls will revel in their newfound powers and glance around the room with a sly grin.

You can start your entry into sneaky tricks and resourcefulness here.

SPY Girl

Science can be difficult to understand but you can demonstrate its principles with common household items. Paper and cardboard from product packaging, paper clips, aluminum foil, and paper cups can be quickly transformed into practical science projects.

If you're curious about the sneaky adaptation possibilities of more complex household devices, this is the book for you. People frequently throw away damaged gadgets and toys without realizing they can serve unintended purposes. If you want to practice recycling and learn high-tech resourcefulness, the following projects will provide plenty of fun product-reuse applications.

Using items found around the house, you will be able to create a sneaky vest, a note copier, invisible ink, how to make a sneaky tracing machine and a periscope, and more.

You will also learn unlikely sneaky hiding places, sneaky codes and ciphers, and how to detect counterfeit currency.

All of the projects are all tested safe and can be made in no time.

Hide and Sneak:
Secure Valuables in Everyday Things

You've seen movies where a character hides something at home and you think, That's the first place I'd look! Well, this project will illustrate how to choose sneaky locations that are the last places a Man of Steal would look. You don't always have access to a safe deposit box or the time to install alarms on all of your possessions. But you can find sneaky hide-in-plain-sight places to frustrate and waste a thief's time.

Selecting this hiding place generally depends on two factors: the size of the item and the frequency of access required. From a package of soap to a tennis ball, a typical home offers a variety of clever hiding places, as shown in **Figure 1**. Wrapping your valuables in black plastic bags will further prevent discovery.

With enough time, a tenacious thief can eventually find virtually anything you hide. That's why you should have a room entry alarm installed in combination with sneaky hiding places to reduce the time a thief will spend searching for your valuables.

More Hide and Sneak

When you think of sneaky you usually think of something that is secret or hidden from you. Actually, the most common sneaky-use application is hiding your valuable belongings from others.

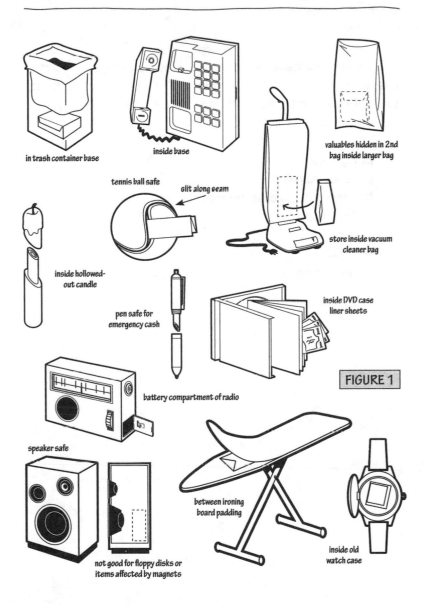

in trash container base

inside base

valuables hidden in 2nd bag inside larger bag

tennis ball safe

slit along seam

store inside vacuum cleaner bag

inside hollowed-out candle

pen safe for emergency cash

inside DVD case liner sheets

FIGURE 1

battery compartment of radio

speaker safe

between ironing board padding

inside old watch case

not good for floppy disks or items affected by magnets

The following ideas can be used to keep your things to yourself, even if they are in plain sight. Most likely a thief or nosy houseguest will briefly examine the item and then ignore it as a possible safe. See the list below for more examples.

- Figurine
- Tissue container
- Video or audio cassette shell
- Inner pocket
- Shoestring
- Between magazine pages
- Inside a candy box

Detect Counterfeit Currency

Whether it's a hundred-dollar bill or a one, getting stuck with counterfeit money is a fear many of us have. In the United States in 2002, $43 million in fake currency was circulated. When counterfeit currency is seized, neither consumers nor companies are compensated for the loss. So what can we do about it? This project describes two methods to tell good currency from bad.

The first method is a careful visual inspection of the bill. Compare a suspect note with a genuine note of the same denomination and series. Look for the following telltale signs:

1. The paper on a genuine bill has tiny red and blue fibers embedded in it. Counterfeit bills may have a few red and blue lines on them but they are printed on the surface and are not really embedded in the paper.

2. The portrait and the sawtooth points on Federal Reserve and Treasury seals are distinct and clear on the real thing.

3. The edge lines of the border on a genuine bill are sharp and unbroken.

4. The serial number on a good bill is evenly spaced and printed with the same color as the Treasury seal.

The second way to verify paper currency is to test the ink. How can we do this in a sneaky way, at home or in the office? Easy: by using one important feature of the ink used on U.S. currency. A legitimate bill has iron particles in the ink that are attracted to a strong magnet. To verify a bill, obtain a very strong magnet or a rare-earth magnet. Rare-earth magnets are extremely strong for their small size. They can be obtained from electronic parts stores and scientific supply outlets. See the Resources section at the back of this book.

You can also use small refrigerator magnets, connecting them end to end to create collectively a much stronger single magnet. See **Figure 1**.

What's Needed
▶ Dollar bill
▶ Strong magnet

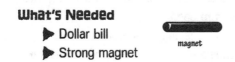

magnet

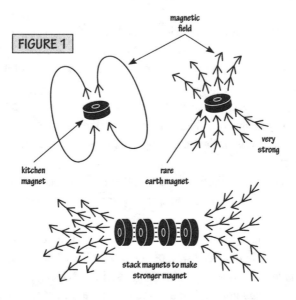

FIGURE 1

magnetic field

kitchen magnet

rare earth magnet

very strong

stack magnets to make stronger magnet

What to Do

Fold the bill in half crosswise and lay it on a table, as shown in **Figure 2**. Point the strong magnet near the portrait of the president on the bill, but do not touch it. A legitimate bill will move toward the magnet, as shown in **Figure 3**.

Whenever you doubt the authenticity of paper currency, simply pull out your magnet and perform the magnetic attraction test.

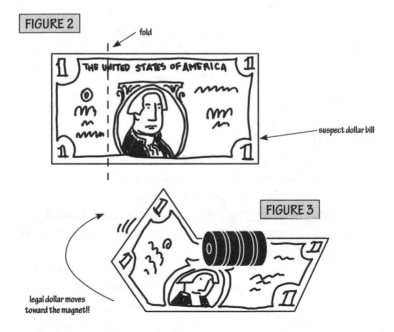

FIGURE 2

fold

THE UNITED STATES OF AMERICA

suspect dollar bill

FIGURE 3

legal dollar moves
toward the magnet!!

Sneaky Tracing Machine

Some items cannot be copied using a chemical transfer technique because their images are printed on coated paper or, in the case of text, the image will be reversed.

Another way to make a duplicate of an original image is to use a Sneaky Tracer.

What's Needed

▶ Four cardboard strips
▶ Hole punch or nail
▶ Paper clips
▶ Paper-clip box
▶ Tape
▶ Two pencils

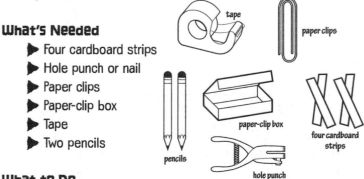

tape

paper clips

pencils

paper-clip box

four cardboard strips

hole punch

What to Do

First, cut two pieces of cardboard, each measuring 2 by 8 inches. Then cut another two pieces, each 2 by 4 inches.

Arrange the cardboard pieces in the pattern shown in **Figure 1** and then punch holes in the corners of the shape. Bend paper clips into C shapes and push them through the holes to secure the pieces, yet still allow them to move freely.

Next, punch pencil-sized holes in the cardboard at points A and B, just large enough so a pencil can fit through snugly, and insert a pencil in each (see **Figure 2**). Now place the copier device so one end rests on the top of the paper-clip box and secure it with tape.

The box acts as an elevated mounting platform to keep the pencils balanced and stable yet free to move about.

Last, select an original drawing that you want to trace and set it under the pencil in hole A. Place a blank sheet of paper under hole B. Use pencil A to trace the drawing and you'll see another picture being created by pencil B. If necessary, secure the pencils to the cardboard and the paper to the table with tape. See **Figure 3**.

Now you can easily trace complex drawings and make copies for your needs. Experiment with the lengths of cardboard, and you'll see that you can easily enlarge or reduce the size of the drawings made.

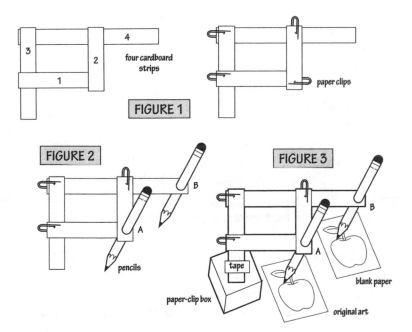

Sneak Peeks around Corners with a Periscope

One of the most useful devices you can build is a periscope, which allows you to take sneak peeks around corners or over fences without being seen. A periscope uses two mirrors positioned so light is reflected from the top mirror down to the lower mirror.

This project illustrates how to construct your own sneaky periscope in no time using an ordinary food carton and a couple of mirrors or watch batteries.

What's Needed

long cardboard box

tape

scissors

two watch batteries

- ▶ Two small mirrors or watch batteries
- ▶ Long cardboard food box, typically 8 inches long and 1 inch wide
- ▶ Transparent tape
- ▶ Scissors

What to Do

First, unfold the food container box and lay it flat as shown in **Figure 1**.

Next, cut two 1-inch square holes in the box as shown in **Figure 2**. Cut one hole close to the top end of section 1 and cut the other hole near the bottom edge of section 3.

At the opposite ends of the holes in sections 1 and 3, fold over

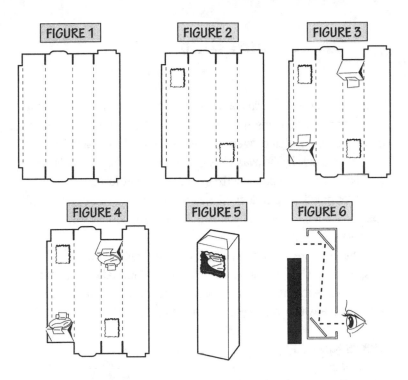

the flaps to form triangles and secure them to the box with tape. See **Figure 3**. These flaps will act as mirror mounts.

Position the mirrors (or watch batteries) on the triangular flaps so they are leaning toward the center of the cardboard and secure them with tape as shown in **Figure 4**.

Last, fold the box so it's back to its original form. Secure the seams and ends with tape. See **Figure 5**.

When you hold the periscope upright, as shown in **Figure 6**, you will be able to see over tall obstructions without being seen. When you hold the periscope sideways, you will be able to see around corners.

Wild, Wild Vest

The following project will illustrate how you can modify a favorite vest to access your favorite items and sneaky devices for a variety of purposes. You can mix and match different gadget sets according to your "mission." You're limited only by the availability of devices and your imagination.

The various vest-accessorizing examples that follow were selected for practicality. If desired, you can outfit your sneaky vest with a personal siren alarm, mini voice recorder, a retractable key ring, and a camera.

When you are traveling, the vest can be outfitted with a compass, mini poncho, pocket heater, mini survival kit, telescope, and a defensive repellent sprayer. You'll no doubt develop more personal creations that will express your mood and personality.

What's Needed

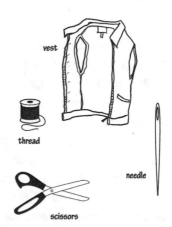

- Vest
- Cloth that matches the vest's interior color
- Scissors
- Needle
- Thread
- Velcro strips or dots with sticky tape backing

vest

thread

needle

Optional:

- Personal alarm

scissors

- Retractable key ring
- Whistle
- Compass
- Mini mirror (from a compact makeup kit)
- LED blinking lights
- Camera
- Superthin, protective poncho
- Mini voice recorder
- Mini telescope

personal alarm

LED

camera

compass

What to Do

Select a vest, preferably with a collar, made from sturdy material. A blue jean vest fits the bill perfectly. With some extra denim from a pair of old, discarded jeans, and a needle and thread, you can add sneaky pockets for personal items, such as a superthin, protective poncho.

FIGURE 1

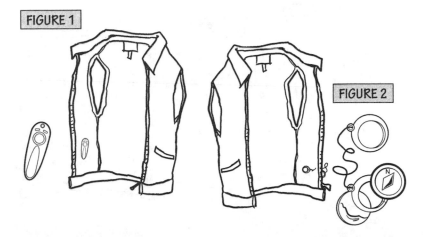

FIGURE 2

For safety, apply Velcro strips to the inside of the vest and to a personal alarm. Select the type that includes a cord that hangs so when it's pulled, the alarm blasts an ultraloud squeal. Allow the cord to hang just below the inside waist for easy access, as shown in **Figure 1**.

You can clip or sew a retractable key ring to the vest and attach a whistle, compass, mirror, and other devices to the vest, using the ring. Items may also be attached with Velcro dots applied directly to the vest. See **Figure 2**.

For fun, apply Velcro dots or strips to the vest so you can add LED blinking lights or your desired emblems and initials (ready-made from a store cut from spare fabric). This allows you to change your look when the mood strikes. See **Figure 3**.

The vest pockets can hold other valuable sneaky items, including a mini digital camera, superthin poncho, mini voice recorder, and mini telescope, as shown in **Figure 4**.

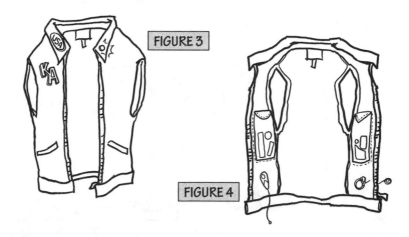

FIGURE 3

FIGURE 4

Collared

The Wild, Wild Vest's lapel or a favorite jacket's collar provides a great hiding place for your favorite sneaky items.

Follow the accessorizing directions below, but remember that you can also add to your sneaky vest other items that are not shown here.

What's Needed

vest

flexible flashlight

▶ Vest or jacket
▶ Velcro strips with sticky tape backing
▶ Flexible flashlight
▶ Two small magnets
▶ Small mirror
▶ Mini voice recorder

What to Do

First, attach two small Velcro squares on each side of the lapel of your vest or jacket. This will allow you to quickly position and mount a variety of miniature devices that are available for your eyes and ears. Simply apply the other half of each Velcro strip, by its sticky backing, to the items of your choice.

For example, as shown in **Figure 1**, you can mount a small flashlight with a flexible end, to have hands-free illumination when needed.

Want to see behind you while walking down the street, talking on your cell phone, or opening a door? Glue a small magnet on the side of the flexible light's end and another onto a small mirror. Mount the mirror on the end of the shaft. This will provide you with an adjustable mount for a sneaky rearview mirror. See **Figure 2**.

Figure 3 illustrates how a mini voice recorder can be mounted under the collar, giving you the ability to secretly record important conversations.

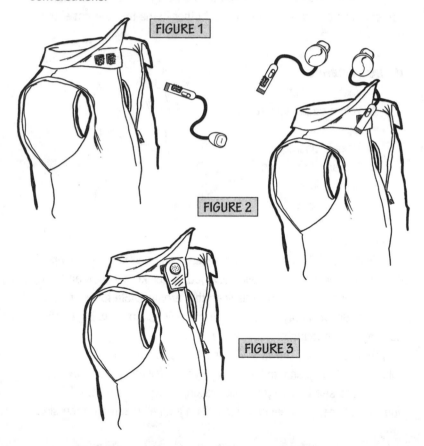

FIGURE 1

FIGURE 2

FIGURE 3

Sneaky Buttons

Virtually every area of your sneaky vest can be used for sneaky sub-
terfuge. Even the buttons can be used to conceal miniature sneaky
devices, as you'll see in this fun project.

What's Needed

- Retractable key ring
- Needle
- Thread
- Button cover kit
- Strong magnet
- Small mirror

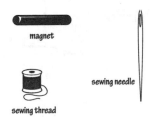

magnet

sewing thread

sewing needle

What to Do

Obtain a button cover kit from a sewing supply store. The kit
should include a button base and a snap-on cover, which when as-
sembled leaves a hollow space inside the button. This allows you to
conceal small items, such as a folded sheet of paper with emergency
numbers and personal passwords. Also, a small, strong magnet inside
the button will come in handy, as you'll see below.

Attach the end of a mini retractable key ring to the inside of the
vest and sew it to the button loop through the vest's button hole, as
shown in **Figure 1**. Insert the magnet in the button base and press
on the cover to complete the button. See **Figure 2**.

Whenever you doubt the authenticity of paper currency, simply pull
out your button magnet and perform the following magnetic attraction

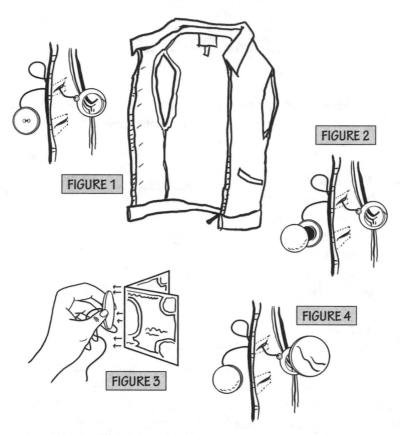

FIGURE 1

FIGURE 2

FIGURE 3

FIGURE 4

test: Fold the bill in half and hold it up in the air. Bring the button, with the magnet inside, near the edge of the bill but do not touch it. A legitimate bill will move toward the magnet. See **Figure 3**.

If desired, you can stick a small mirror onto the other side of the key ring. When you want to discreetly see behind you without alerting onlookers, simply pull the key ring so you can have a clear rear view. See **Figure 4**.

Sneaky Backpack

Your backpack is a constant companion and, as such, should be outfitted with crucial items for emergency situations. While you're at it, go ahead and add some nice accessories, for a personal touch.

This project will illustrate unique add-ons you can apply to your backpack, using items you probably already have.

What's Needed

▶ Backpack

Optional:

▶ Mini flexible flashlight
▶ Lightweight foil-backed thermal blanket
▶ Hand warmer
▶ Mini fan
▶ Velcro dots with sticky tape backing
▶ Old folding umbrella shaft with handle
▶ Toy car chassis (with wheels)
▶ Personal alarm
▶ Walkie-talkie
▶ Tape
▶ Voice recorder

backpack

flexible flashlight

mini fan

umbrella

toy car

walkie-talkie

FIGURE 1

FIGURE 2

What to Do

Add an over-the-shoulder flexible flashlight to illuminate your way, hands free, as shown in **Figure 1**.

For emergencies, it's always good to have on hand a lightweight foil-backed thermal blanket (which can even serve as a tent), hand warmer, and mini fan. **Figure 2** illustrates how you can setup an emergency, heated "home away from home," using an old umbrella shaft. Here's how:

Apply Velcro dots to the cloth base of an old folding umbrella shaft and extend the handle. Then apply four Velcro dots to the top of an old toy car's chassis. Apply Velcro dots to the sides and bottom of

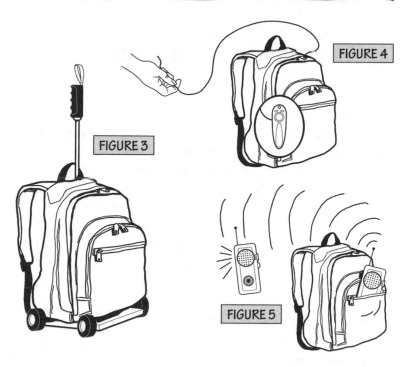

FIGURE 4

FIGURE 3

FIGURE 5

the backpack. Press the car to the bottom of the backpack and the umbrella to the side. See **Figure 3**.

Using a personal alarm, you can set your backpack down and walk away from it. As shown in **Figure 4**, if someone takes the backpack away, the alarm will sound to alert you.

Even when you're away from the backpack, it can serve a purpose as a listening device if you hide a walkie-talkie inside with its TALK button taped down. You can listen from a distance with the other walkie-talkie, as shown in **Figure 5**. Or use a tape recorder, with its RECORD button taped down, to record secretly from inside the backpack.

Sneaky Sugar Glass

When you see a character in a TV show or movie crash through a window, it's not really glass they are breaking. Special effects men use a sheet of clear substance that's actually made of sugar!

You can make your own fake glass for models and hobby projects like they do in the movies. All you need are a few common kitchen items.

What's Needed

- Butter
- Nonstick pan or baking sheet
- One cup of sugar
- Nonstick frying pan
- One tablespoon of water

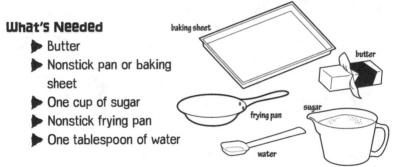

baking sheet

butter

frying pan

sugar

water

What to Do

First, spread a thin layer of butter on the surface of the baking sheet and let it cool for one hour in the refrigerator. Then, pour a cup of sugar into the frying pan, add a tablespoon of water, and place the pan on a stove-top burner. Turn the heat on low. See **Figures 1, 2,** and **3**.

Next, stir the sugar continually so it will not burn. It will liquefy when heated. See **Figure 4**. When the sugar is completely liquefied but before it starts to turn brown, remove the baking sheet from the refrigerator and pour the sugar onto it, as shown in **Figure 5**. (Be sure to turn off the heat, and to allow the pan to cool on an

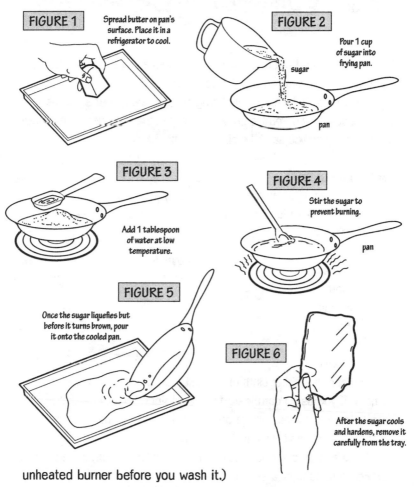

FIGURE 1 Spread butter on pan's surface. Place it in a refrigerator to cool.

FIGURE 2 Pour 1 cup of sugar into frying pan.

sugar

pan

FIGURE 3 Add 1 tablespoon of water at low temperature.

FIGURE 4 Stir the sugar to prevent burning.

pan

FIGURE 5 Once the sugar liquefies but before it turns brown, pour it onto the cooled pan.

FIGURE 6 After the sugar cools and hardens, remove it carefully from the tray.

unheated burner before you wash it.)

Let the sugar cool and you will have a sheet of fake glass that you can use for hobby models and other projects. See **Figure 6**.

Sneaky Undercover Camera Cozy

Who hasn't wanted to snap a picture of an amazing or embarrassing sight, but didn't want to attract attention?

If you'd like to take sneaky photographs on the go but are too shy, this project's for you. You'll learn how to disguise your camera in a sneaky cozy covering so you can take pictures without being spotted.

What's Needed

- Small digital camera
- Small, clean juice box or other food container
- Tape
- Scissors
- Cloth
- Needle
- Thread

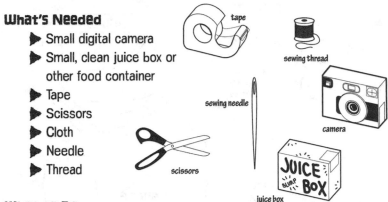

tape

sewing thread

sewing needle

camera

scissors

juice box

What to Do

You can use either cloth or a small food container to hide the camera. If you use a cardboard food container, select one that is slightly larger than the camera and cut holes in it for the shutter button and lens, as shown in **Figure 1**.

Figure 1 also shows a box you can construct from a piece of cardboard to conceal a slim camera.

Alternatively, you can cut a piece of fabric that is about ½ inch longer and wider than the camera and sew it into a camera cozy. See **Figure 2**.

Now you can secretly take pictures anytime you wish, without attracting attention. See **Figure 3**.

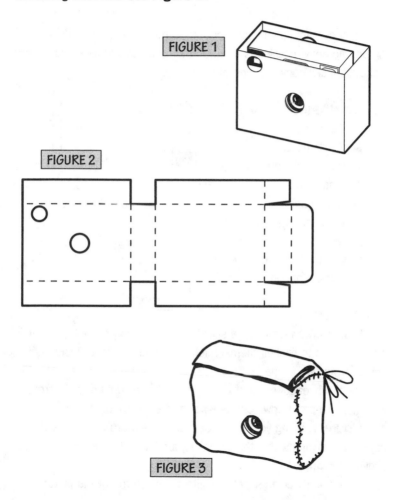

FIGURE 1

FIGURE 2

FIGURE 3

Sneaky Copier

Have you ever found yourself needing to make a copy of a drawing and no copy machine is around? Using household items you can make a sneaky copy machine of your own.

What's Needed

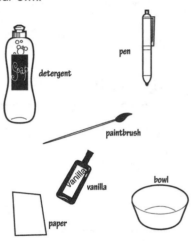

- ► Teaspoon
- ► Vanilla extract
- ► Liquid dish detergent
- ► Small bowl
- ► White paper
- ► Ink pens of various colors
- ► Paintbrush (optional)
- ► Comic strip or newspaper picture (optional)

What to Do

First, draw a picture on a sheet of paper, using a black pen. Go over the lines to thicken them. (Thicker lines allow you to make more copies from the original.)

Next, mix equal parts of vanilla extract and liquid dish detergent together in a small bowl; one teaspoon of each should be enough; see **Figure 1**. Using your finger or a small paintbrush, completely cover the drawing with a thin layer of your Sneaky Copier solution, as shown in **Figure 2**.

Now place a clean sheet of white paper on top of the picture.

Rub the back of the paper firmly with the bowl of the teaspoon until the picture begins to show through the paper. Peel the paper off the picture to see your copier creation; see **Figure 3**. You should be able to make multiple copies this way if your original drawing has thick dark lines.

Last, test the Sneaky Copier technique with other ink colors. Try to make a copy of a newspaper page or a comic strip. Keep in mind that the images on the copy will be reversed.

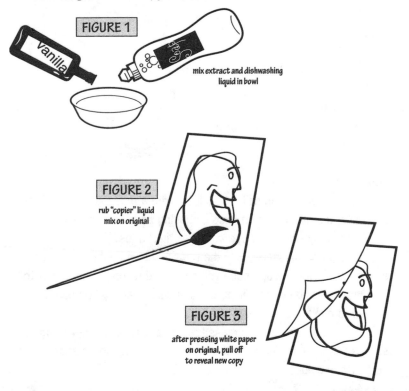

FIGURE 1

mix extract and dishwashing liquid in bowl

FIGURE 2

rub "copier" liquid mix on original

FIGURE 3

after pressing white paper on original, pull off to reveal new copy

Invisible Ink

If anything is a prime example of a Sneaky Use project, it's using everyday things to make invisible ink. (Sneaky fact: Casinos now use cards marked with symbols that are only visible when viewed with a special lens.) You can use a large variety of liquids to write secret messages. In fact, some prisoners of war used their own saliva and sweat to make invisible ink.

What's Needed

bowl

lemon juice

paper

cotton swabs

▶ Milk or lemon juice or equal parts baking soda and water
▶ Small bowl
▶ Cotton swab or toothpick
▶ Paper

What to Do

Use a cotton swab or toothpick to write a message on white paper, using the milk or lemon juice or baking soda solution as invisible ink. The writing will disappear when the "ink" dries.

To view the message, hold the paper up to a heat source, such as a lightbulb. The baking soda will cause the writing in the paper to turn brown. Lemon or lime juice contain carbon and, when heated, darken to make the message visible.

You can also reveal the message by painting over the baking soda solution on the paper with purple grape juice. The message will be bluish in color.

Sneaky Invisible Ink II

Here's another sneaky method to write and view invisible messages that stay invisible (unless you know the trick), this time using common laundry detergent and water.

What's Needed

bowl

white cardboard

detergent

cotton swabs

- Cotton swab or towel
- Small bowl
- Liquid detergent
- Water
- Black light
- Piece of white cardboard

What to Do

In a small bowl, mix a teaspoon of liquid laundry detergent with one cup of water and use a small towel or cotton swab to write a message on a white piece of cardboard. See **Figure 1**. The message will not be visible at this point.

To view the secret message, darken the room and shine a black light—invisible ultraviolet light—on the board. The previously invisible message will become visible, as shown in **Figure 2**.

write secret message with swab

FIGURE 1

black light reveals secret message

FIGURE 2

Sneaky Book for girls

WOMEN ICONS

Here are just a few of the women who have positively impacted our society. Their achievements in a wide range of areas are a great source of inspiration.

JANE GOODALL

Jane Goodall is celebrated for her forty-five-year study of chimpanzee social and family interactions in Gombe Stream National Park, Tanzania. She also founded the Jane Goodall Institute.

Interested in animals from her youth, Goodall encouraged notable anthropologist Louis Leakey to hire her as his assistant. Along with Biruté Galdikas, who advanced studies in orangutans, and Dian Fossey, famous for living with gorillas, Goodall made major strides in primate research by observing them unobtrusively from within their own habitat.

LINDSAY DAVENPORT

Lindsay Davenport has been the World's No. 1 American professional tennis player four times, winner of three Grand Slam singles tournaments as well as an Olympic gold medal in singles, and recipient of more prize money than any other professional female athlete.

Davenport is also the tallest female Grand Slam titleholder, at slightly over 6 feet 2 inches (1.89 m). She attributes some of her success to self-confidence, having had to overcome both shyness and self-consciousness about her height, which had initially hampered her game when she was in her teens.

JANET GUTHRIE

Janet Guthrie, born in 1938, was the first woman to qualify and compete in both the Indianapolis 500 and the Daytona 500. She started out as an aerospace engineer but began racing in 1963.

In 1976, Guthrie became the first woman to compete in a NASCAR Winston Cup superspeedway race, the World 600, in which she finished fifteenth. Guthrie raced in the Daytona 500 and the Indy 500 the following season, and in numerous NASCAR and Indy races during the next several years.

She was inducted into the International Motorsports Hall of Fame in 2006, and her suit and helmet are now preserved at the Smithsonian Institution.

MARIE CURIE

Marie Curie led the way in the field of radioactivity. She is the first woman to be awarded a Nobel Prize, and the only person ever to win the award in two different sciences, physics and chemistry, in 1903 and 1911, respectively, as well as one of only two people to win two Nobels in different fields (Linus Pauling is the other). Her daughter, Irène Joliot-Curie, would also win a Nobel Prize, in chemistry.

Born Maria Skłodowska, Marie was the first female professor at the University of Paris, where she taught physics, and the first Frenchwoman to be awarded a doctorate, in mathematics.

She met her husband, Frenchman Pierre Curie, through their mutual interest in the magnetic qualities of steel. In 1898, the couple named the first new radioactive chemical element that they discovered, "polonium," for Marie's native country, Poland. Later that year, the Curies revealed the existence of another element, radium; it is they who coined the term "radioactivity" to describe the qualities of these elements.

Marie Curie's invention of portable radiology units was a boon for wounded soldiers during World War I. She later headed the Pasteur Institute and, in 1932, founded the Radium Institute, now the Maria Skłodowska-Curie Institute of Oncology, in her hometown of Warsaw.

JULIA CHILD

Julia Child was a famous author, cook, and television host who introduced Americans to French cuisine and cooking techniques. It all began in 1961, when she wrote the now classic cookbook *Mastering the Art of French Cooking*. Her TV series, *The French Chef*, premiered two years later on PBS, and won the first Emmy for an educational program.

Many cooks are unaware that she had volunteered with the American Red Cross and, in 1941, joined the Office of Strategic Services (OSS), a predecessor to the CIA. For a year, she worked at the OSS Emergency Sea Rescue Equipment Section in Washington, D.C., where she assisted in the development of a shark repellent that ensured sharks would not explode ordinance-targeting German U-boats.

After the war, she lived in Paris, where she attended Le Cordon Bleu and with Simone Beck and Louisette Berthold, went on to found a more informal cooking school for Americans living in France, which they called L'École des Trois Gourmands (School of the Three Gourmands). This led to the writing of her landmark first book, published at a time when French cooking was considered foreign and difficult for American homemakers.

As the result of its success, Child would become the featured chef in a dozen television series, as well as make guest appearances on numerous other shows, and publish nearly two dozen books. She received the Presidential Medal of Freedom in 2000. Now every year boasts the presentation of Julia Child Cookbook Awards to other writers who have followed in her footsteps.

MARY KIES

In 1809, Mary Kies received the first patent ever granted to a woman by the U.S. Patent Office for a technique of weaving straw with silk and thread.

Although the Patent Act of 1790 permitted people, regardless of gender, to file for a patent, in most U.S. states women could not own property independent of their husbands or have any legal power to sign contracts. It was therefore almost unthinkable for a woman to apply for a patent for her own work.

Although Kies was not the first to come up with a novel way of weaving straw with silk and thread, to strengthen it, she was the first to patent the technique, which would be applied in the construction of bonnets, saving the American women's hat-making industry during a period when an embargo on foreign materials had caused it to falter.

MARY ANDERSON

Mary Anderson is the inventor of the windshield wiper. Back in 1902, she noticed that motorcar drivers had to leave their windshields down to be able to see during inclement weather. She sought a way to keep the windshields up and the rain and snow out, and invented an automatic car window-cleaning device controlled from inside the car, which was granted as her first patent in 1903 (before Henry Ford patented the Model T). Although she received royalties for its construction by manufacturers, the wipers didn't catch on initially.

Ironically, it was only after her seventeen-year patent ran out in 1920 that Anderson's wiper design became standard equipment on automobiles.

HEDY LAMARR

Hedy Lamarr, born Hedwig Eva Maria Kiesler in Vienna in 1913, achieved fame as a movie actress who also coinvented an early manner of spread-spectrum encoding, significant to modern wireless communication, cordless telephones, WiFi Internet connections, and the cell phone.

On August 10, 1933, she married Friedrich Mandl, an Austrian arms manufacturer, who disapproved of her film career and took her to his business meetings, where she absorbed discussions about military technology.

A neighbor of Lamarr's after she had moved to America, composer George Antheil, also took a keen interest in technology. In 1942, a U.S. patent was granted to Antheil and Hedy Kiesler Markey (Lamarr's real name) for their device that permitted frequency hopping, designed to make it hard for enemies to intercept or jam Allied radio-guided torpedoes. It cleverly used a piano roll to shift among over eighty frequencies. However, the technique was not suitable to the state of technology in 1942.

In 1962, after the patent had expired, it was used by U.S. military ships during the Cuban missile crisis. In 1997, Lamarr was finally recognized for her achievement, when Electronic Frontier Foundation gave her an award for this precursor to modern wireless technology.

MÁRIA TELKES

Maria Telkes, born in 1900, was a Hungarian-American scientist and inventor who created the first thermodynamic generator (1947) and the first thermodynamic refrigerator (1953).

Telkes was awarded her PhD in physical chemistry in Hungary, and then moved to the United States where, from 1939 to 1953, she was involved in solar energy research at Massachusetts Institute of Technology...thereby earning the nickname the "Sun Queen."

Among her other achievements, during World War II, she invented a device that used solar power to convert saltwater to freshwater; in 1948, she designed the heating system for the first solar-powered home. In the 1950s, she came up with solar ovens, which led to a method of using the sun to dry crops.

In 1977, she was honored by the National Academy of Science Building Research Advisory Board for her many achievements.

LOUISA MAY ALCOTT

Louisa May Alcott was an American novelist now best known for *Little Women*, published in 1868 and loosely based on her childhood.

While she was growing up in Massachusetts, her education was rounded out by family friends Henry David Thoreau, Ralph Waldo Emerson, Nathaniel Hawthorne, and Margaret Fuller, as well as instruction by her father, Amos Bronson Alcott, who participated for a time in an experimental utopian project that involved self-sustained living off the land. She found early employment as a teacher and a nurse, but was interested in writing from an early age.

In addition to her well-known, determinedly wholesome works for girls, Alcott also wrote racier novels and stories under the pseudonym A. M. Barnard. These works, still in print today, feature powerful female characters involved in adventures or mysteries, in the vein of what her *Little Women* character Jo attempted to publish of her own works.

SUSAN B. ANTHONY

Susan B. Anthony was a American civil rights leader in the nineteenth-century movement to secure women's suffrage in the United States.

Anthony was a gifted child who learned to read and write at age three; she also learned about civil rights at an early age from her abolitionist father and progressive-minded mother.

The first American women's rights convention took place in 1848, in Seneca Falls, New York. Three years later, she was introduced to another suffragist, Elizabeth Cady Stanton, with whom she organized the first American state temperance society. The two women traveled around the country to promote their causes. Anthony's platform focused on the fact that the 15th Amendment to the U.S. Constitution gave black men the right to vote but omitted any mention of women. With Stanton, in 1869, she founded the National Women's Suffrage Association, to later become the National American Woman Suffrage Association. She died fourteen years before passage of the 19th Amendment, which gave American women the right to vote.

For her advancements of women's rights, Anthony was the first genuine American woman (the allegorical "Liberty" doesn't count) to be honored on a U.S. coin, the Susan B. Anthony dollar. Her life is also the basis for an opera by Gertrude Stein and Virgil Thomson, called *The Mother of Us All*.

STEPHANIE L. KWOLEK

Stephanie L. Kwolek's studies of high-performance aramid fibers led to the invention of Kevlar, the superstrong material used world wide in body armor, safety helmets, and hiking and camping gear; skis, tires, racing sails, canoes, and spacecraft; and fiber-optic cable, mooring, and suspension bridge cables.

As a child, Kwolek was encouraged by her father to learn about nature by exploring the woods around her home. She originally wished to attend but couldn't afford to go to medical school, and instead took a job as a research chemist at the Dupont Company to work at their textile fibers laboratory, where she specialized in studying how to create petroleum-based synthetic fibers of tremendous rigidity and strength.

In 1965, she discovered a new kind of fiber made from polymers that, upon refinement, was "stiffer than glass and very hard to cut with scissors," she said.

Ten years later, the first Kevlar bulletproof vests were sold. Today, this fabric has hundreds of uses and has saved thousands of lives. It is light yet strong—five times stronger than steel—rigid, is flame and corrosion resistant, doesn't wear out with use, and is nonconductive.

On her own or as part of a research team, Kwolek has been granted twenty-eight U.S. patents and became a member of the National Inventors Hall of Fame in 1995.

CHIEN-SHIUNG WU

Chien-Shiung Wu is called the "Madame Curie of China" for her expertise in the field of radioactivity.

Born in Shanghai in 1912, daughter of a progressive father who believed in equal education for women, Wu studied and taught in China and then went to the United States to acquire a PhD in physics at the University of California–Berkeley in 1940. She went on to teach at Smith College, Princeton University (where she was the first woman instructor in the physics department), and Columbia University, and in 1942 married fellow physicist Luke Yuan.

At Columbia, she helped to improve Geiger counters and also worked with the Manhattan Project on a process to isolate the U-235 form of uranium from the more common U-238. Her book *Beta Decay* remains a bible for nuclear physicists. She won her greatest fame, however, for her work with cobalt in disproving the conservation of parity (symmetry) of cells.

In later years, she turned her attention to pinpointing what causes sickle-cell anemia. She has been awarded numerous medals and honorary degrees for her advances in cell research.

Wu's son, Vincent Yuan, has followed in his parents' footsteps, and works as a physicist at the Los Alamos laboratory.

MILDRED "BABE" DIDRIKSON ZAHARIAS

Mildred "Babe" Didrikson Zaharias is perhaps the most versatile female athlete of all time, having successfully competed in the areas of golf, basketball, and track and field.

Born Mildred Ella Didrikson, in Port Arthur, Texas, in 1911 (although she later claimed her birth year was 1914) she first began competing as a seamstress, winning a sewing prize at the 1931 Texas State Fair. Her skill in organized baseball earned her the nickname "Babe." She married wrestler George Zaharias in 1938.

In addition to baseball, Zaharias excelled in track and field, basketball, softball, diving, roller-skating, and bowling. At the 1932 Los Angeles Summer Olympics, she won two gold medals (in javelin and hurdles) and one silver (for high jump).

Zaharias went on to become the first famous female American golfer, winning a never-broken record of seventeen amateur victories in a row. Between amateur and professional matches, she has won eighty-two golf tournaments, and even had one named for her: the Babe Zaharias Open Tournament of Beaumont, Texas.

Fly Girl

Few of our inventions have proved as tantalizing as flying machines. But, ask the average person how they work and whoever you speak to is usually stumped.

This section will illustrate how airplanes and helicopters fly and how you can easily demonstrate this phenomenon with everyday items. You'll learn how to quickly assemble an origami flying Frisbee and additional gliders from ordinary paper, and make working boomerangs from discarded food cartons and mini boomerangs from postcards.

You'll also learn about noteworthy women of aviation history. With the information provided, girls will take the wind out of the sails of boys that believe aviation is exclusively a male subject.

How Planes Fly

Have you ever wondered how airplanes and helicopters are able to fly? If you have, and want to demonstrate this principle, all you need are such ordinary items as straws, postcards, and strips of paper.

Air Pressure Demonstration I

An ordinary straw can be used to demonstrate that air pressure is all around us (15 pounds per square inch, to be exact). You can demonstrate this easily enough with everyday items.

What's Needed

straw

glass of water

- ▶ Straw
- ▶ Glass filled with water

What to Do

Insert a straw into the glass of water, as shown in **Figure 1**. Next, place a finger over the top of the straw and lift it out of the water. See **Figure 2**.

You'll see that the water stays in the straw and doesn't flow out because air pressure from the bottom is keeping it in, as shown in **Figure 3**. When you lift your finger from the top of the straw, air pressure flows from the top and pushes against the water, forcing it out.

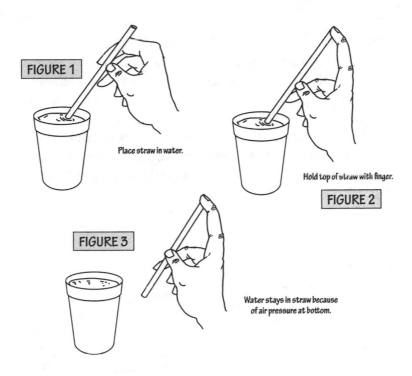

FIGURE 1

Place straw in water.

Hold top of straw with finger.

FIGURE 2

FIGURE 3

Water stays in straw because
of air pressure at bottom.

Air Pressure Demonstration II

You can demonstrate the power of air pressure in a more dramatic way with the following project, again using everyday items.

What's Needed

▶ Glass filled to the brim
   with water
▶ Plastic-coated postcard

postcard

glass of water

What to Do

Working over a sink, hold up the glass of water. Place a postcard over the mouth of the glass and turn the glass upside down, holding the postcard in place with your finger under it, as shown in **Figure 1**.

Carefully remove your finger from the postcard and you should see that the postcard will not fall. With no air in the glass to push against the postcard, the air outside presses against the postcard, keeping it in place, even with the weight of the water upon it. See **Figure 2**.

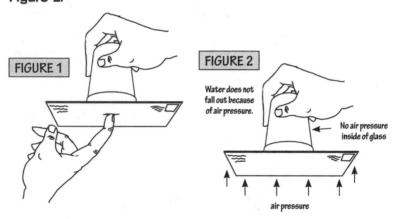

Air Pressure Demonstration III

What's Needed

▶ Paper (preferably a paper towel or napkin)

▶ Scissors

scissors

paper towel

What to Do

Cut a paper strip ½ inch wide by 4 inches in length as shown in **Figure 1**. Hold the paper strip up to your face above your mouth and blow. The paper naturally moves upward. Now hold the paper strip just below your lips and blow above the strip. As shown in **Figure 2**, the paper will also rise and move upward!

This occurs because of Bernoulli's principle, which states that fast-moving air has less pressure than nonmoving air. The air under the strip has more pressure than the air above it and pushes the strip upward.

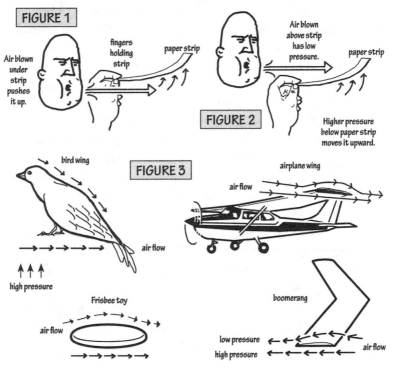

Figure 3 illustrates a side view of a bird's wing, an airplane wing, a Frisbee flying disk, and a boomerang. Notice the top of the wing curves upward and has a longer surface as compared to the bottom. When the airplane moves forward, air moves above and below the wing. The air moving along the curved top must travel farther and faster than the air moving past the flat bottom surface. The faster-moving air has less pressure than the air at the bottom and this provides lift.

Baseball pitchers can take advantage of Bernoulli's principle by releasing the ball with a forward spin. The ball produces a lower pressure below it, causing it to dip when it reaches the plate. Hence, a curveball. See **Figure 4**.

Sailboats apply Bernoulli's principle to use the wind, regardless of its direction, to propel the boat in any desired direction. **Figure 5** shows how altering the shape of the sail into a curve produces an effect similar to that of an airplane wing. The wind moves at a faster rate over the curved side, with a lower pressure, and the higher pressure on the other side of the sail pushes the boat laterally. A centerboard, attached to the boat hull, prevents the boat from moving sideways while allowing it to use the wind thrust to move forward. See **Figure 6**.

Automobile bodies are similar to an airplane wing because they are flat on the bottom and curved on top. They can lose stability at high speeds since they tend to achieve lift from the higher air pressure below, as shown in **Figure 7**. To reduce the Bernoulli effect, automakers have incorporated improvements in vehicle design, such as lowering the body height, adding special front bumper and fender contours, and installing rear spoilers. See **Figure 8**.

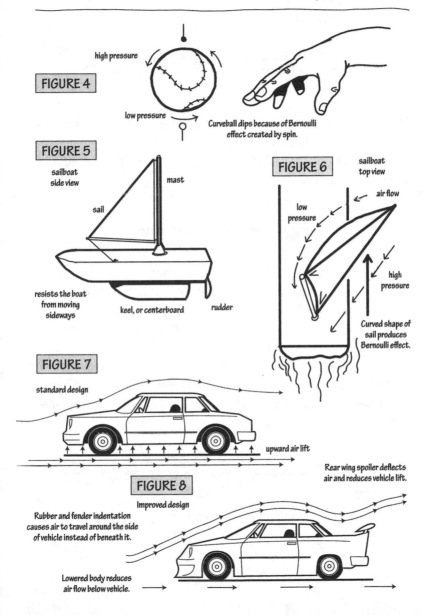

FIGURE 4

high pressure

low pressure

Curveball dips because of Bernoulli effect created by spin.

FIGURE 5

sailboat side view

mast

sail

resists the boat from moving sideways

keel, or centerboard   rudder

FIGURE 6

sailboat top view

air flow

low pressure

high pressure

Curved shape of sail produces Bernoulli effect.

FIGURE 7

standard design

upward air lift

Rear wing spoiler deflects air and reduces vehicle lift.

FIGURE 8

Improved design

Rubber and fender indentation causes air to travel around the side of vehicle instead of beneath it.

Lowered body reduces air flow below vehicle.

Eye to the Sky

To the untrained eye, nearly all aircraft look alike. But Sneaky Fly Girls should be able to shout out the names of popular aircraft used in movies, TV shows, and by local police departments. It's not hard if you know what to look for.

Parts of an Airplane

Figure 1 illustrates the parts of a jet airplane. It will help you identify the necessary components that allow an aircraft to generate thrust, lift, and change direction.

The body of a plane (the center of the aircraft that accommodates the crew, passengers, and cargo) is called the *fuselage*. A jet engine generates thrust to move the aircraft forward and is mounted in an enclosure called a *nacelle*. The wings generate lift. At the rear of the plane you'll find the *tail fin*, the *vertical stabilizer*, and a smaller wing called the *horizontal stabilizer*.

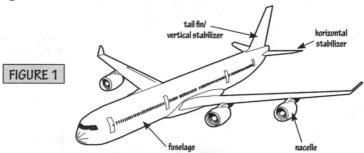

tail fin/
vertical stabilizer

horizontal
stabilizer

FIGURE 1

fuselage

nacelle

The pilot controls the rudder and elevators to move the plane to the left and right, and up and down. The airplane wings have movable parts on them, allowing the plane to roll, or tilt, and to alter the lift of the plane, during takeoff, or to create drag during landing.

If you look closely at an aircraft's fuselage shape, as well as at the number of engines (or rotors) and their locations, it's easy to determine one craft from another.

The top twelve most distinctive aircraft in use today are included in **Figures 1** through **10**. By studying the distinguishing features in the following illustrations, you'll be able to easily identify helicopters, commercial aircraft, and military airplanes in no time.

Commercial Airplanes

Boeing/McDonald Douglas DC-10 or MD-11—It is a large craft with one engine under each wing and a third mounted on the tail section. See **Figure 1A**.

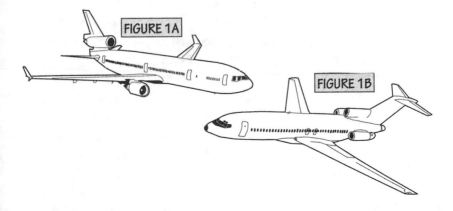

Boeing 727—Another large plane with three engines. You can tell it apart from the DC-10 or MD-11 by noticing the engine locations and the tail fin. It has two engines mounted at the rear of the fuselage and a third on the distinctive "T" tail fin. See **Figure 1B**.

Airbus A340/A380—A very large airplane. It is, along with the Boeing 747, the only commercial aircraft with two engines under each wing. The A380 is larger than the A340. Here's how they compare: **Airbus 340**: length 59.39 m (194 ft 10 in), wingspan 60.30 m (197 ft 0 in); **Airbus A380**: length 73 m (239 ft 6 in), wingspan 79.8 m (261 ft). See **Figure 2**.

Boeing 747—A very large airplane. In addition to being the only other large commercial aircraft with two engines on each wing (besides the Airbus A340/A380), it has a distinctive bulge in the front upper fuselage, for the first-class section. See **Figure 3**.

Military Airplanes

Boeing E-3 AWAC—This four-engine plane, with two under each wing, has a very large disk, which can be seen from all angles, on the rear fuselage, for its unique airborne warning and control system (airborne radar-tracking system). See **Figure 4**.

Lockheed F-117 Stealth—This unique wedge design is used to deflect radar for virtually invisible-to-radar reconnaissance missions. See **Figure 5**.

Harrier VTOL—Look for a midfuselage engine aircraft that directs flow to the wings for a vertical takeoff and landing (like a helicopter). Note the large rectangular air scoops on either side of the aircraft. See **Figure 6**.

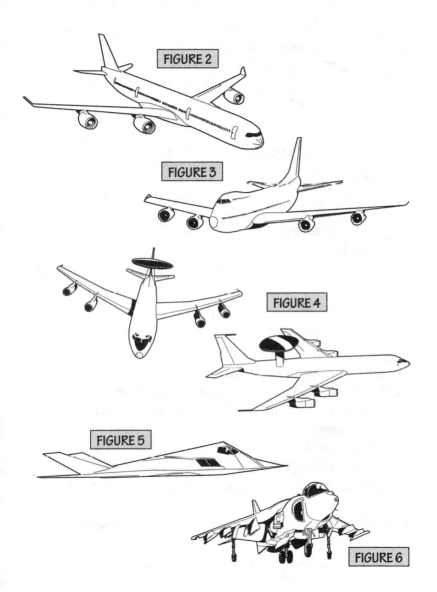

FIGURE 2

FIGURE 3

FIGURE 4

FIGURE 5

FIGURE 6

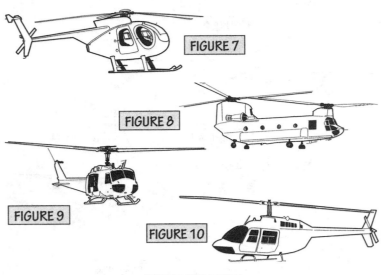

FIGURE 7

FIGURE 8

FIGURE 9

FIGURE 10

Helicopters

Hughes 500—This small helicopter is easily recognized by its egg-shaped fuselage. See **Figure 7**.

Boeing Chinook—A large copter with two rotors. The fuselage has a raised rear section, so the rotors won't collide, which gives it a banana shape. See **Figure 8**.

Bell "Huey" UH-1—Nicknamed the "Huey" because its original designation was HU-I. This medium-size helicopter has a sleek appearance with a wide body. Seen frequently in war movies. See **Figure 9**.

Bell JetRanger—Very popular with TV stations and police departments, the medium-size JetRanger has a sleek appearance and a narrow body. See **Figure 10**.

Sneaky Frisbee

You've seen how Bernoulli's principle works. Now it's time to put it to use and make a sneaky flyer, similar to flying disk toys, using paper and tape.

What's Needed

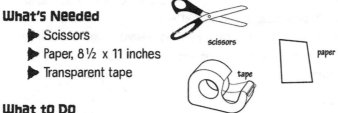

scissors

paper

tape

▶ Scissors
▶ Paper, 8½ x 11 inches
▶ Transparent tape

What to Do

Cut eight 2-inch square pieces of paper as shown in Figure 1. Fold the top right corner of one square down to the lower left corner. See **Figure 2**. Then, fold the top left corner down to the bottom, as shown in **Figure 3**.

Repeat these two folds with the remaining seven squares. See **Figure 4**.

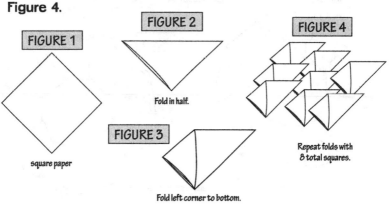

FIGURE 1

square paper

FIGURE 2

Fold in half.

FIGURE 3

Fold left corner to bottom.

FIGURE 4

Repeat folds with 8 total squares.

Insert one paper figure into the left pocket of another, as shown in
Figure 5. Repeat inserting the figures into one another until they form
an eight-sided doughnut shape; see **Figure 6**. Apply tape as needed
to keep the origami flyer together and turn over, as shown in **Figure 7**.

Next, bend up the outer edge of the sneaky flyer to form a lip, as
shown in **Figure 8**. This outer lip will cause the air to take a longer
path over it, producing a Bernoulli effect.

Turn the device so the lip is bent downward. Throw the Sneaky
Frisbee with a quick snap of your wrist and it should stay aloft for a
great distance.

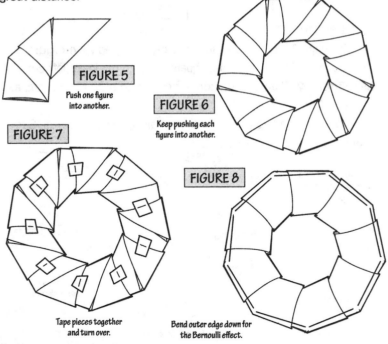

FIGURE 5

Push one figure
into another.

FIGURE 6

Keep pushing each
figure into another.

FIGURE 7

Tape pieces together
and turn over.

FIGURE 8

Bend outer edge down for
the Bernoulli effect.

Sneaky Boomerang

Want a sneaky way to play catch alone? You just need a piece of
cardboard and foam rubber to make a working boomerang that will
actually fly up to 30 feet away and return.

What's Needed

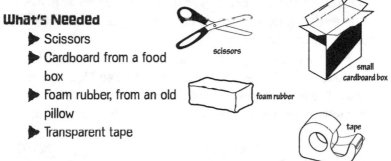

scissors

small
cardboard box

foam rubber

tape

- ▶ Scissors
- ▶ Cardboard from a food
  box
- ▶ Foam rubber, from an old
  pillow
- ▶ Transparent tape

What to Do

Cut the cardboard into the boomerang shape shown in **Figure
1**. Each wing of the boomerang should be 9 inches long by 2 inches
wide.

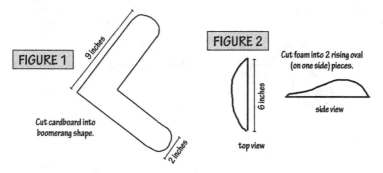

FIGURE 1

9 inches

2 inches

Cut cardboard into
boomerang shape.

FIGURE 2

Cut foam into 2 rising oval
(on one side) pieces.

6 inches

top view

side view

Then, cut two foam pieces into 6 by 2-inch oval shapes with one side rising into a curve. The rising shape should resemble the side view of an airplane wing. See **Figure 2**. Place the oval foam pieces on the leading edges of the boomerang and secure them with tape.

Note: Look carefully at the placement of the ovals on the boomerang wings in **Figure 3** before taping them. The foam creates a curved shape on the boomerang wing, which will cause air to move faster across its top than across the bottom surface. This will produce lift for the boomerang.

Hold the boomerang as if you were going to throw a baseball and throw it straight overhead (not to the side). See **Figure 4**. The Sneaky Boomerang should fly straight and return to the left. Experiment with different angles of throw to obtain a desired return pattern.

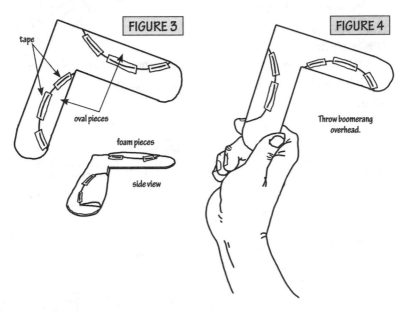

FIGURE 3

tape

oval pieces

foam pieces

side view

FIGURE 4

Throw boomerang overhead.

Sneaky Mini-Boomerang

You can use postcards, business cards, or cardboard food boxes to make a miniature, palm-size boomerang that actually flies and returns to you, for indoor fun.

What's Needed

▶ Scissors
▶ Cardboard from food boxes or postcards

scissors

small cardboard box

What to Do

Cut out the boomerang shapes shown in **Figure 1**. The boomerang wings can be any length between 2 to 4 inches. For optimal flight height and return performance, cut each wing of the boomerang 2½ inches long and ½ inch wide.

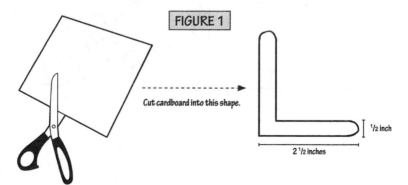

FIGURE 1

Cut cardboard into this shape.

½ inch

2 ½ inches

Set the Sneaky Mini-Boomerang on the palm of your raised hand with one wing hanging off. Tilt your hand slightly upward. With your other hand's thumb and middle finger ½ inch away, snap the outer boomerang wing. You'll discover (after a few attempts) that it will fly forward and return to you. See **Figure 2**.

Note: You must snap your finger with a strong snapping action to make the boomerang fly away and return properly, as shown in **Figure 3**.

Experiment with different hand positions and angles to control the boomerang's flight pattern.

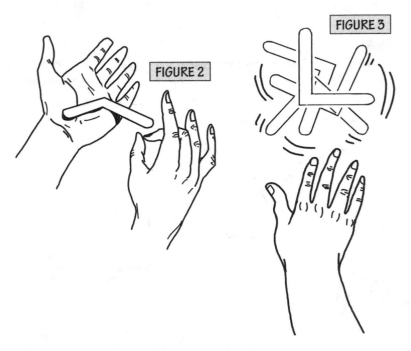

FIGURE 2

FIGURE 3

Sneaky Glider

You don't have to spend money on a balsa wood kit to make a simple working glider. A working glider, made from discarded cardboard or Styrofoam material, can produce plenty of sneaky flyers for safe fun.

What's Needed

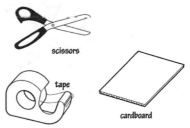

- Scissors
- Flat corrugated cardboard or Styrofoam
- Transparent tape

scissors

tape

cardboard

What to Do

The Sneaky Glider body, or fuselage, can be cut out from the pattern shown in **Figure 1**. The plane will require at least one wing near the center for stability. A smaller wing near the rear rudder can also be added. Simply insert the wing(s) into the body slits and use tape to secure them properly as shown in **Figure 2**.

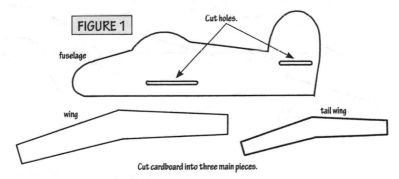

FIGURE 1

Cut holes.

fuselage

wing

tail wing

Cut cardboard into three main pieces.

Launch the Sneaky Glider with a snap of the wrist near your ear and it should fly up to 30 feet away. See **Figure 3**. Test the glider wing(s) shapes to achieve various flight paths as desired.

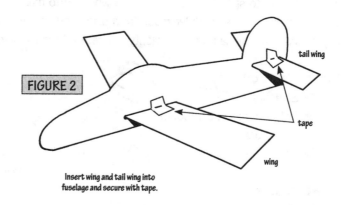

FIGURE 2

tail wing

tape

wing

Insert wing and tail wing into
fuselage and secure with tape.

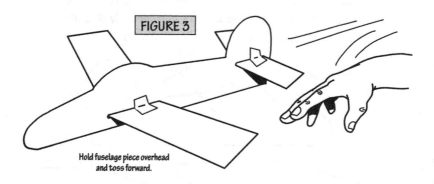

FIGURE 3

Hold fuselage piece overhead
and toss forward.

WOMEN AVIATORS

EILEEN M. COLLINS

Eileen M. Collins was the first female pilot and also the first commander of a U.S. space shuttle. In 1995, she piloted mission STS-63, when it made a vital rendezvous between the *Discovery* and the Russian space station *Mir*. For this achievement, she received the Harmon Trophy.

In 1999, she was the commander of the *Columbia* mission STS-93 to deploy the Chandra X-ray Observatory telescope.

She also commanded the 2005 mission STS-114, which carried supplies to the International Space Station. During this mission, she became the first astronaut to complete a 360-degree pitch maneuver of *Discovery*.

She retired from NASA in 2006, and has since become a familiar face on CNN, working as an analyst of shuttle launches and landings.

HARRIET QUIMBY

Harriet Quimby was the first woman to earn a U.S. pilot's certificate as well as the first woman to fly across the English Channel.

She originally worked as a journalist and theater critic, and wrote five screenplays for romantic silent film shorts directed by D. W. Griffith for Biograph Studios.

After attending the Belmont Park International Aviation Tournament in 1910, she became interested in flying, attended flight school, and passed the pilot's test in 1911; classmate Matilde Moisant was to become America's second certified female aviator the following year.

In 1912, Quimby became the first woman to pilot a plane from Dover to Calais, making the crossing in just under an hour. Unfortunately, her achievement received little press because the *Titanic* had sunk a day earlier.

In 1991, she was honored on a U.S. postage stamp.

BESSIE COLEMAN

Bessie Coleman, nicknamed "Queen Bess," was the first African American pilot, and the first American of any race or gender to hold an international pilot license.

Tenth of thirteen siblings, the part-Cherokee Coleman had to walk four miles to her Atlanta, Texas, school each day, but excelled at reading and mathematics. Her father was to abandon the family. Determined to make something of herself in a day when many woman of any race did not even finish high school, Coleman, enrolled in the Oklahoma Colored Agricultural and Normal University, but could only afford to attend it for one year.

At age twenty-three, she found work as a manicurist at a barber shop with a well-respected clientele. Hearing stories from her clients about flying in World War I, Coleman began to dream of becoming a pilot. She could not gain admission to American flight schools because she was black and a woman, but one of the clients, black newspaper publisher Robert Abbott, suggested she study abroad.

Coleman studied French at the Berlitz school in Chicago, then headed for Paris, where she learned to fly in a biplane. On June 15, 1921, Bessie Coleman became the first African American woman to earn an international aviation license from the Fédération Aéronautique

Internationale, and the first African American woman in the world to earn an aviation pilot's license.

She traveled to Holland and Germany to meet aircraft designer Andrew Fokker and to obtain additional training at his factory. She returned to the United States to quickly make a name for herself as a daredevil ace pilot, performing stunts at air shows. Refusing to lower her dignity for the sake of additional fame, she turned down a film offer that would have depicted her early life in a manner she felt was racist.

Danger Girl

Every girl can learn how to become resourceful in minutes, using nothing but a few items fate has put at her disposal. When you're in a bind, the best answer is frequently not the obvious one. Sometimes you have to be sneaky.

You will learn little-known methods to make wire and batteries in a pinch, how to use everyday items as weapons, easily escape a grasp, and how to make a compass. You'll also learn simple direction-finding methods, memory tricks, and how to setup a simple door or drawer alarm.

Also included are sneaky projects that show how to modify toys and candy package accessories into useful alarms and security devices.

With the projects and techniques in this section, you will be ready to improvise simple security devices and safety gear in a pinch. You, too, can do more with less!

Parts and Crafts

Ordinary wire can be used in many sneaky ways. You'll soon learn how it can be utilized to make a radio transmitter, a speaker, and more.

When wire is required for sneaky projects, whenever possible try to use everyday items that you might otherwise have thrown away. Recycling metal will help save our natural resources.

Getting Wired

In an emergency, you can obtain wire—or items that can be used as wire—from some very unlikely sources. **Figure 1** illustrates just a few of the possible items that you can use in case connecting wire is not available.

Ready-to-Use Wire can be Obtained from:
- Telephone cords
- TV/VCR cables
- Headphone wire
- Earphone wire
- Speaker wire
- Wire from inside toys, radios, and other electrical devices

Note: Some of the sources above will have one to six separate wires inside.

Wire for projects can also be made from:

▶ Take-out food container handles
▶ Twist-ties
▶ Paper clips
▶ Envelope clasps
▶ Ballpoint pen springs
▶ Fast-food wrappers
▶ Potato chip bag liners

You can also use aluminum from the following items:

▶ Margarine wrappers
▶ Ketchup and condiment packages
▶ Breath mint container labels
▶ Chewing gum wrappers
▶ Trading card packaging
▶ Coffee creamer container lids

Note: The wire used from the sources above are only to be used for low-voltage, battery-powered projects.

FIGURE 1

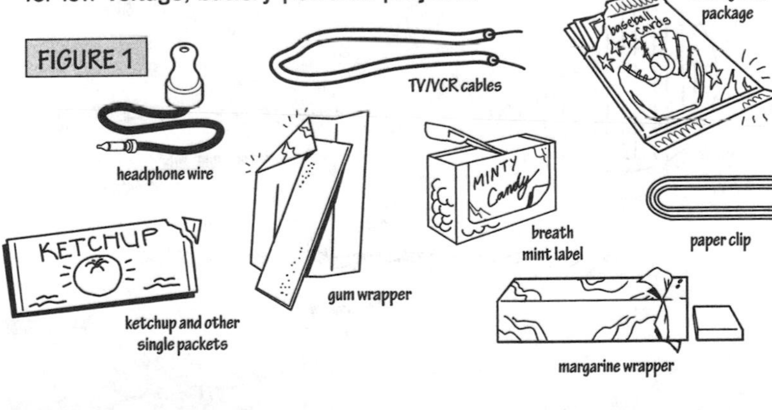

trading card package

TV/VCR cables

headphone wire

breath mint label

paper clip

KETCHUP

gum wrapper

ketchup and other single packets

margarine wrapper

Use special care when handling fragile aluminum materials. In some instances, aluminum may be coated with a wax or plastic coating that you may be able to remove.

You can cut strips of aluminum material from food wrappers easily enough. With smaller items—such as aluminum obtained from a coffee creamer container—use the sneaky cutting pattern shown in **Figure 2**.

Making resourceful use of items to make sneaky wire is not only intriguing, it's fun.

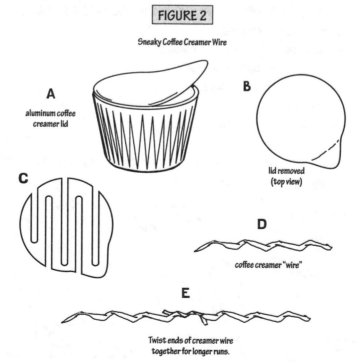

FIGURE 2

Sneaky Coffee Creamer Wire

A

aluminum coffee
creamer lid

B

lid removed
(top view)

C

D

coffee creamer "wire"

E

Twist ends of creamer wire
together for longer runs.

Make Batteries from Everyday Things

No one can dispute the usefulness of electricity. But what do you do if you're in a remote area without AC power or batteries? Make sneaky batteries, of course!

In this project, you'll learn how to use fruits, vegetable juices, paper clips, and coins to generate electricity.

What's Needed

▶ Lemon or other fruit
▶ Nail
▶ Heavy copper wire
▶ Paper clip or twist-tie
▶ Water
▶ Salt
▶ Paper towel
▶ Pennies and nickels
▶ Plate

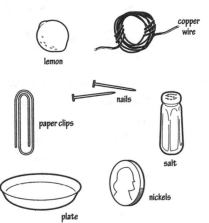

copper wire

lemon

nails

paper clips

salt

nickels

plate

What to Do
The Fruit Battery

Insert a nail or paper clip into a lemon. Then stick a piece of heavy copper wire into the lemon. Make sure that the wire is close to, but does not touch, the nail (see **Figure 1**). The nail has become the battery's negative electrode and the copper wire is the positive electrode. The lemon juice, which is acidic, acts

FIGURE 1

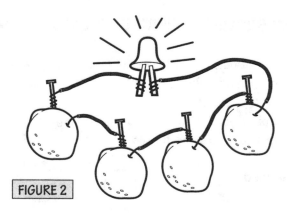

FIGURE 2

as the electrolyte. You can use other item pairs besides a paper clip and copper wire, as long as they are made of different metals.

The lemon battery will supply about one-fourth to one-third of a volt of electricity. To use a sneaky battery as the battery to power a small electrical device, like an LED light, you must connect a few of them in a series, as shown in **Figure 2**.

The Coin Battery

With the fruit battery, you stuck the metal into the fruit. You can also make a battery by placing a chemical solution between two coins.

Dissolve 2 tablespoons of salt in a glass of water. This is the electrolyte you will place between two dissimilar metal coins.

Now moisten a piece of paper towel or tissue in the salt water. Put a nickel on a plate and put a small piece of the wet absorbent paper on the nickel. Then place a penny on top of the paper (see **Figure 3**).

In order for the homemade battery to do useful work, you must make a series of them stacked up as seen in **Figure 4**.

Be sure the paper separators do not touch one another.

The more pairs of coins you add, the higher the voltage output will be. One coin pair should produce about one-third of a volt. With six pairs stacked up, you should be able to power a small flashlight bulb, LED, or other device when the regular batteries have failed. *Power will last up to two hours.*

Once you know how to make sneaky batteries, you'll never again be totally out of power sources.

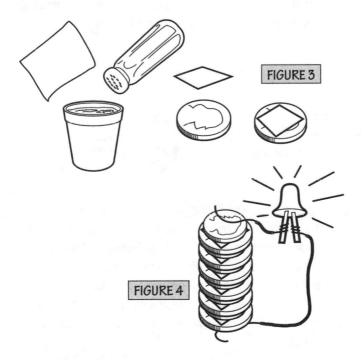

FIGURE 3

FIGURE 4

Craft a Compass

If you're ever lost, you'll find a compass is a crucial tool. When markers or trails are nonexistent, a compass can keep you pointed in the right direction to get you back to a line of reference.

A compass indicates Earth's magnetic north and south poles. For a situation where you are stranded without a compass, this project describes three ways of making one with the things around you. For each method, you will need a needle (or twist-tie, staple, steel baling wire, or paper clip); a small bowl, cup, or other nonmagnetic container; water; and a leaf or blade of grass. How simple is that?

Method 1

What's Needed

▶ Magnet—from a radio or car stereo speaker

stereo speaker

What to Do

Take a small straight piece of metal (but do not use aluminum or yellow metals), such as a needle, twist-tie, staple, or paper clip, and stroke it in one direction with a small magnet. Stroke it at least fifty times, as shown in **Figure 1**. This will magnetize the needle so it will be attracted to Earth's north and south magnetic poles.

Fill a bowl or cup with water and place a small blade of grass or any small article that floats on the surface of the water. Place the

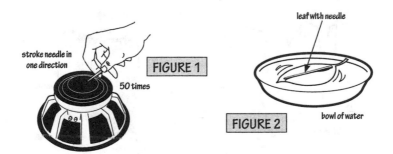

stroke needle in
one direction

FIGURE 1

50 times

leaf with needle

FIGURE 2

bowl of water

needle on the blade of grass (see **Figure 2**) and watch it eventually
turn in one direction. Mark one end of the needle so that magnetic
north is determined.

Note: To verify the north direction, see the next section,
Direction-Finding Methods.

Method 2

What's Needed

▶ Silk or synthetic fabric—
from a tie, scarf, or other
garment

silk tie

What to Do

As in the first method, stroke a needle or paper clip in one direction with the silk material. This will create a static charge in the metal,
but it will take many more strokes to magnetize it. Stroke at least
300 times, as shown in **Figure 3**. Once floated on a leaf in the bowl,

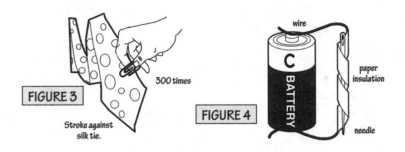

FIGURE 3

300 times

Stroke against
silk tie.

FIGURE 4

wire

paper
insulation

needle

the needle should be magnetized enough to be attracted to Earth's
north and south magnetic poles. You may have to remagnetize the
sneaky compass needle occasionally.

MethOd 3

What's Needed
► Battery
► Wire
► Staple/paper clip

wire

battery

paper clip

What to Do
When electricity flows through a wire, it creates a magnetic field.
If a small piece of metal, like a staple, is placed in a coil of wire, it
will become magnetized.

Wrap a small length of wire around a staple or paper clip and connect
its ends to a battery, as shown in **Figure 4**. If the wire is not insulated,
wrap the staple with paper or a leaf and then wrap the wire around it.

When you connect the wire to the battery in this manner, you are creating a short circuit—an electrical circuit with no current-draining load on it. This will cause the wire to heat quickly so only connect the wire ends to the battery for short four-second intervals. Perform this procedure fifteen times.

Place the staple on a floating item in a bowl of water, and it will eventually turn in one direction. Mark one end of the staple so that magnetic north is determined.

Direction-Finding Methods

If you're stranded without a magnetic compass, all is not lost. Even without a compass, there are numerous ways to find directions in desolate areas. Two methods are covered here.

Method 1: Use a Watch

What's Needed
▶ Standard analog watch
▶ Clear day where you can
see the sun

watch

What to Do
The sun always rises in the east and sets in the west. You can use this fact to find north and south with a standard nondigital watch.

If you are in the Northern Hemisphere (north of the equator), point the hour hand of the watch in the direction of the sun. Midway between the hour hand and 12 o'clock will be south. See **Figure 1**.

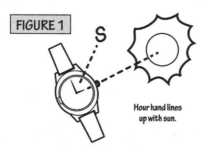

FIGURE 1

S

Hour hand lines
up with sun.

MethOd 2: USe The StarS

UJhat's Needed

▶ A clear evening when stars can be viewed

UJhat tO DO

In the Northern Hemisphere, locate the Big Dipper constellation in the sky; see **Figure 2**. Follow the direction of the two stars that make up the front of the dipper to the North Star. (It is about four times the distance between the two stars that make up the front of the dipper.) Then follow the path of the North Star down to the ground. This direction is north.

In the Southern Hemisphere, locate the Southern Cross constellation in the sky; see **Figure 3**. Also notice the two stars below the Cross. Imagine two lines extending at right angles, one from a point midway between the two stars and the other from the Cross, to see where they intersect. Follow this path down to the ground. This direction is due south.

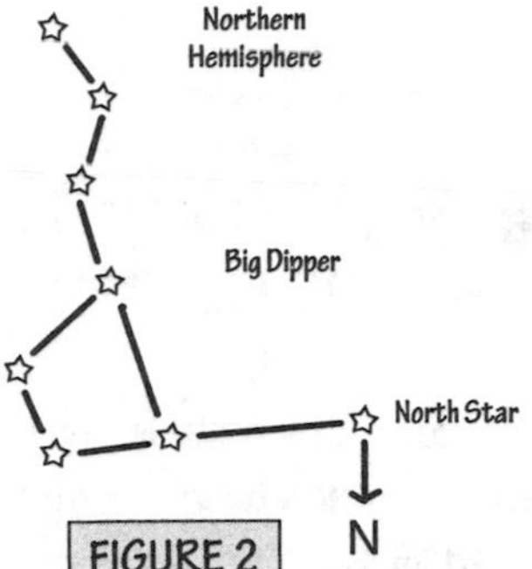

FIGURE 2   N

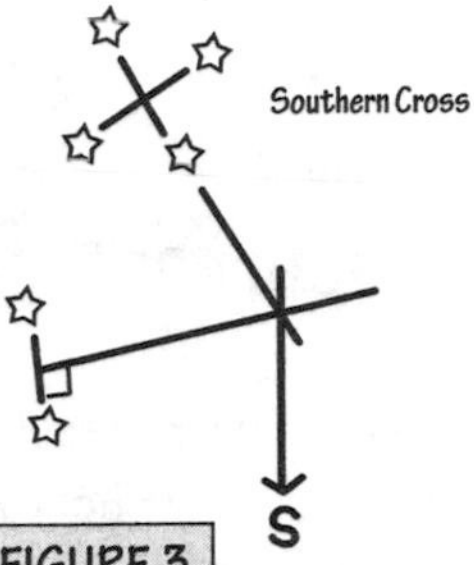

FIGURE 3   S

Longitude and Latitude

Latitude

Latitude represents how far north or south you are, relative to the equator. When you're at the equator, your latitude is zero. The North Pole's latitude is 90 degrees north. Conversely, the South Pole is 90 degrees south.

Note: South latitude figures, which are south of the equator, are represented as negative numbers.

Longitude

Longitude represents how far east or west you are, relative to the Greenwich meridian. Places to the west of Greenwich have longitude angles up to 180 degrees west. Positions east of Greenwich have longitude angles up to 180 degrees east. Longitude west figures are input as negative numbers.

Decimal and Degrees/Minutes/Seconds Notation

Maps and GPS receivers show latitude and longitude angles. Maps usually show bold lines marked in degrees (whole numbers) plus possibly intermediate lines marked 15, 30, 45 minutes or 10, 20,

30, 40, 50 minutes. GPS receivers typically show degrees plus minutes and decimal fractions of a minute (e.g., 45 : 23.1234).

Each degree can be subdivided into 60 minutes (and each minute into 60 seconds for very high precision).

In cases where the map (or GPS readout) is in degrees and minutes, convert the minutes to decimals of a degree by dividing the number of minutes by 60. **For example:**

50 deg 30 minutes north = 50.5 degrees

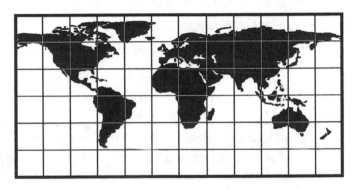

For example: Anchorage, Alaska, 61 13 149 54 = 61 degrees, 13 minutes north and 149 degrees, 54 minutes west. Degrees are sometimes represented with a ° symbol and minutes with a ' symbol. A typical notation looks like this: Anchorage, Alaska 61° 13' N 149° 54' W.

You can design and play a city location quiz by using a world map and listing only the coordinates from the list below—be sure to leave out the city names. Place the proper city names in an answer key to make a sneaky quiz.

For example, here is a sample quiz you can try:

1. Which city is 41° 50' N 87° 37' W at 11:00 A.M.?

2. Which city is 42° 21' N 71° 5' W at 12:00 noon?

3. Which city is 40° 47' N 73° 58' W at 12:00 noon?

4. Which city is 33° 45' N 84° 23' W at 12:00 noon?

Answers: 1. Chicago, Ill., 2. Boston, Mass., 3. New York, N.Y., 4. Atlanta, Ga.

Cities	Latitude	Longitude (decimal and degrees/minutes)	Time
(**Example:** Chicago, Ill. 41° 50' N 87° 37' W at 11:00 A.M. Notice that all of the cities below are degrees north and degrees west because they are all in North America.)			
Anchorage, Alaska	61° 13' N	149° 54' W	8:00 A.M.
Atlanta, Ga.	33° 45' N	84° 23' W	12:00 noon
Baltimore, Md.	39° 18' N	76° 38' W	12:00 noon
Boise, Idaho	43° 36' N	116° 13' W	10:00 A.M.
Boston, Mass.	42° 21' N	71° 5' W	12:00 noon
Buffalo, N.Y.	42° 55' N	78° 50' W	12:00 noon
Chicago, Ill.	41° 50' N	87° 37' W	11:00 A.M.
Cincinnati, Ohio	39° 8' N	84° 30' W	12:00 noon

Simple Door or Drawer Alarm

Sure, traveling has its charms, but with exotic environments sometimes come mysterious and unexpected dangers. It doesn't happen
often, but when you stay overnight away from home you probably
worry about someone entering your room without your knowledge.
The following projects provide a trio of portable and quick-to-set-up
security gimmicks for use at home, on a trip, or for an unforeseen
stay in a foreign location to thwart or detect window and door break-
ins at a moment's notice.

What's Needed

- Rubber bands
- Bubble-wrap material
- String or wire
- Cardboard
- Small bell or chime

rubber bands

cardboard

string

What to Do

To be warned when someone
enters a room, place bubble-wrap
material under a mat or towel near
the entrance. Or place a small bell
or chime on the door or window
(see **Figure 1**).

Place a chime or bell against
a window handle or on a doorsill

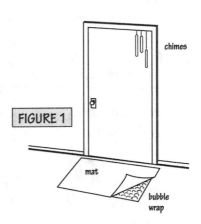

chimes

FIGURE 1

mat

bubble
wrap

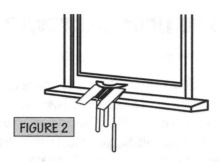

FIGURE 2

so it will produce a loud popping sound when activated (see **Figure 2**).

Optionally, use whatever unbreakable but noisy items are available to place against a door or window to alert you when they are displaced.

How to Prevent Breaking and Entering

What's Needed

- Wire or strong nylon thread
- Broom, mop handle, plunger dowel, or chair
- Towels
- Tape or rubber bands
- Duct tape

rubber bands

wire

broom handle

towel

duct tape

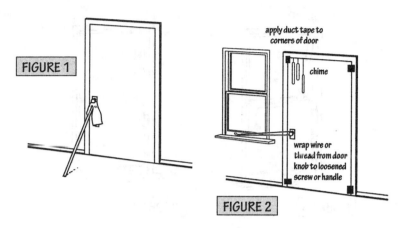

FIGURE 1

apply duct tape to
corners of door

chime

wrap wire or
thread from door
knob to loosened
screw or handle

FIGURE 2

What to Do

To protect a door from opening, place a long object, like a broom, mop, or chair, under the doorknob so it's wedged in tight. If necessary, use towels or small pillows to anchor the object to the floor to prevent slippage (see **Figure 1**).

Even strong nylon thread can prevent a door from opening if it's wrapped tightly from the doorknob to an adjacent window handle or wall light-plate fixture screw. Apply duct tape to all corners of the door to further prevent a break-in (see **Figure 2**).

Similarly, a window can be secured with an object to prevent it from sliding in its track, as shown in **Figure 3**.

If a single long object is not available, use shorter ones, like aerosol cans or slender bottles. Position all of the objects end to end and secure them with tape or rubber bands to keep them in line (see **Figure 4**).

Although a determined burglar can breech these entry inhibitors, they give you valuable time to react and call for help. A chime can be taped to the windows and doors to alert you that a break-in is in progress.

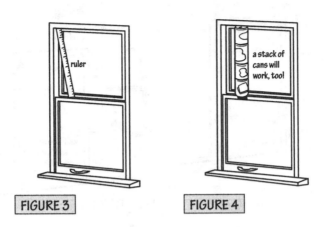

FIGURE 3   FIGURE 4

Phantom Menace Noisemakers

Your home audio/video system is probably your pride and joy. Others might enjoy it too. But they may not spend the time and money shopping at the places you did. They may take the direct-theft route to aural delight.

What's Needed

- Wire
- Aluminum foil
- Cardboard
- Radio, tape recorder, or battery-powered clock radio
- Ballpoint pen spring

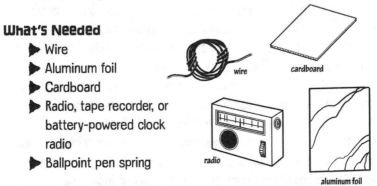

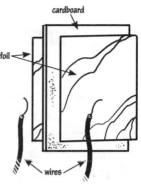

cardboard

foil

wires

What to Do

You can cause a door or window opening to activate a battery-powered radio, a tape player, or a battery-powered alarm clock using a power separator switch and contact sensor. Any battery-powered toy or gadget that makes noise will work. The power separator switch, made from foil, wire, and cardboard as shown in **Figure 1**, is placed between batteries in a radio, tape player, or noise-making toy.

First, tape a piece of aluminum foil at the side of the door near the hinge. Then remove the spring from a ballpoint pen. Tape the spring on an adjacent area, near (but not touching) the aluminum foil strip on the door. Bend and mount the spring so that the door must be open about one third of the way before it touches the foil on the door.

Next, attach wires to the spring and the foil and connect them to the wires on the power separator switch (see **Figure 2**). Now, when the door is opened, the spring contacts the foil, which completes the circuit, allowing the radio or tape player to obtain power from the batteries. Be sure to set the volume high enough to alert you that a door or window has been breeched.

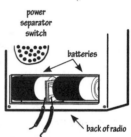

power separator switch

batteries

back of radio

FIGURE 1

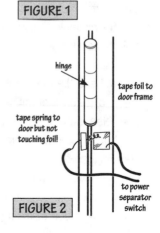

hinge

tape foil to door frame

tape spring to door but not touching foil!

to power separator switch

FIGURE 2

Sneaky Memory Tricks

We all have to memorize information for school, for work, and in our personal life. Some things are easier to remember, while other topics have no apparent link or association, making recall difficult.

The memory-association tips and examples below will illustrate how you can develop your own memory helpers in the future.

Mnemonics

A *mnemonic* is a device that helps you memorize something. It allows you to easily organize and store information in and out of your long-term memory, to give you a handle for its recollection. Mnemonics can be visual, as in a dramatic picture of something, or can be a code word.

For example, if you don't want to forget where you placed your cell phone, use your imagination to create an exaggerated image of your placing the phone on your table. Imagine that the phone is ten feet tall and the table is as large as a two-car garage. Create a huge image of a ten-foot-tall cell phone growing out of the table. Notice what else is on or near the table, and include that in the image.

When you develop your own mnemonics, use positive, exaggerated images that you can relate to. Take the time to associate the thing you want to remember with something that's familiar.

Here are some examples below of mnemonic images and words that will help you develop your own memory helpers:

Sneaky Memory Trick I

FIGURE 1

Figure 1 illustrates the nine planets in our solar system. Use the first letter in the sentence below to help you remember the order of planets from the sun:

My **V**ery **E**arnest **M**other **J**ust **S**erved **U**s **N**ine **P**ickles
**Mercury, Venus, Earth, Mars, Jupiter,
Saturn, Uranus, Neptune, Pluto**

Sneaky Memory Trick II

FIGURE 2

Figure 2 displays the heads on Mount Rushmore. Use the first letter in the sentence below to help you remember the four presidents of the United States on Mount Rushmore.

We **J**ust **L**ike **R**ushmore
Washington, Jefferson, Lincoln, Roosevelt

Sneaky Memory Trick III

Figure 3 showcases a simple illustration to help you remember the proper way to set your clocks and watches during the biannual time change for daylight savings time:

Spring ahead, fall back

FIGURE 3

Sneaky Memory Trick IV

Memorize the sentences below to quickly get the number of days in a month straight:

Thirty days hath September, April, June, and November.
All the rest have 31 (February has 28).

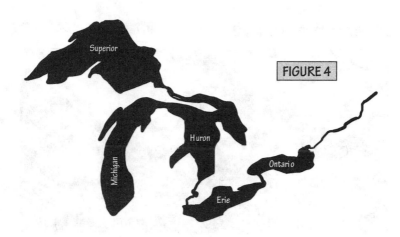

FIGURE 4

Sneaky Memory Trick V

Figure 4 provides a map of the five Great Lakes. Use the mnemonic below to help your recall their names:

H O M E S
Huron, Ontario, Michigan, Erie, Superior

Sneaky Memory Trick VI

It's difficult to remember the complete wave spectrum. To help with this, repeat the memorable sentence below a few times until you can name the order of waves with ease:

Clark **G**able e**X**pects **U**nanimous **V**otes **I**n **M**ovie **R**eviews **T**onight
**Cosmic, Gamma, X-rays, Ultraviolet, Visible, Infrared,
Microwave, Radio, Television**

Sneaky Memory Trick VII

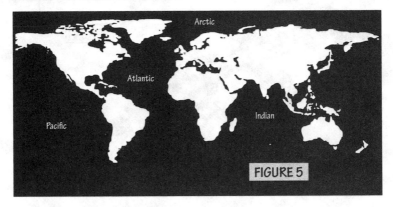

FIGURE 5

Figure 5 illustrates the four oceans of the world. Use this short sentence to help you remember them:

I Am A Person.
Indian, Arctic, Atlantic, Pacific

Bonus Memory Trick:

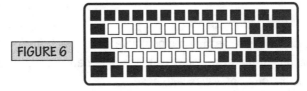

FIGURE 6

Figure 6 shows the keys of a typical keyboard. To quickly test every key, type the following sentence:

The quick brown fox jumps over the lazy dog.

Use Items as Weapons

According to the Bureau of Justice, a violent crime occurs in the United States every five seconds. Being prepared can save your life. You don't need a can of Mace to protect yourself from attackers. In some instances, ordinary objects can be used effectively as weapons.

First, an important warning: Don't contend with adversaries. You won't lose a fight you don't participate in. If you can, run away as soon as possible and yell for help.

In situations where there is no other way out, you will find that common objects, from a public phone to a magazine, can distract an assailant, keep distance between you, and, if you must strike, reduce injury and protect your flesh and bones. Here's how to defend yourself:

Public phone. If an assailant decides to attack you while you're on the phone, use the handset to hit your attacker on the nose or temple. In a phone booth, use the door to wedge the attacker's arm or leg.

Coins. You can throw a handful of coins at an attacker's face to stun and throw him or her off balance. See **Figure 1**.

Pens and pencils. Pens and pencils can be used to jab at an assailant's exposed skin and cause enough of a distraction to enable you to escape.

Magazines. By rolling up a magazine and holding it tight, you can strike the face, temple, or ear to temporarily disable an attacker. See **Figure 2**.

One other technique to remember: If the attack has not occurred but is imminent, hold the ordinary object down in a nonthreatening way. The attacker may not realize that you will use it as a weapon.

If you sense that a threatening situation is escalating, look around, grab whatever you can—your shoes, a book, a cup, a package, a box, a small printer: anything you can throw and use it as if your life depends on it.

FIGURE 1

FIGURE 2

How to Escape a Grasp

When possible, avoid physical confrontation. If necessary, call for help. Throwing punches is futile and dangerous, and in many cases, you injure your hand when you hit the other person. But in some instances, you may be attacked or grabbed without warning. In these situations, you must do something. The following techniques show easy-to-learn escapes that do not require lots of strength and can be quickly mastered.

As shown in **Figure 1**, the weak spot on the hand is between the thumb and forefinger. When an assailant grabs you, you will have a big advantage toward escaping his grasp if you locate this weak spot on his hand.

By pulling or twisting against the weak spot, as shown in **Figures 2** and **3**, you will escape from an assailant's grasp without a lot of effort. Practice this technique with a friend until it's a reflex action.

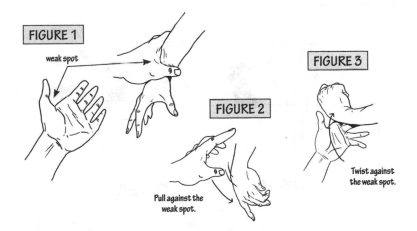

FIGURE 1

weak spot

FIGURE 3

FIGURE 2

Pull against the weak spot.

Twist against the weak spot.

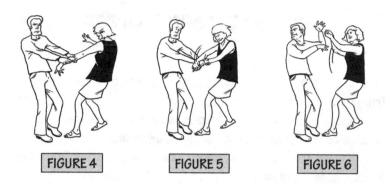

FIGURE 4   FIGURE 5   FIGURE 6

If someone grabs your arm with both hands as shown in **Figure 4**, use your free arm to grab your other hand as shown in **Figure 5**. Then raise both arms and turn (**Figure 6**). This will affect the weak spot on both of the assailant's hands causing him to release his grasp.

Similarly, if an assailant grabs both of your arms, as shown in **Figure 7**, rapidly pull your arms upward to force him to release his grip. See **Figure 8**.

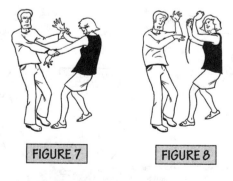

FIGURE 7   FIGURE 8

Recycling Tips

When we use nonrenewable fuel sources, such as coal, natural gas, and oil, it increases the level of carbon dioxide in the atmosphere. Carbon dioxide (CO_2) is a known contributor to the greenhouse effect.

You can take simple steps to reduce waste and the demand for fossil fuels by conserving energy and reducing waste.

Ten Ways You Can Recycle

1. Reduce, Reuse, Recycle

Select reusable products instead of disposables. When you shop, encourage your parents to buy larger quantities and select items with minimal packaging material to help reduce waste. When possible, use rechargeable batteries, and recycle standard batteries, aluminum cans, paper, plastic, and glass. If you recycle just half of your household waste, you could save 2,400 pounds of carbon dioxide annually.

2. Use Less Heat and Air-Conditioning

While at home, ask your parents to lower temperatures to a moderate level. If you set the thermostat just two degrees lower in winter and higher in summer, you can save up to two thousand pounds of CO_2 each year.

3. Change a Light Bulb

If all American households replaced just one incandescent

light bulb with a compact fluorescent light (CFL) bulb, it would eliminate 90 billion pounds of greenhouse gases, the equivalent of taking 7.5 million passenger cars off the road. CFLs can last up to ten times longer than standard bulbs, use one-third of the energy, and give off 70 percent less heat.

4. Drive Less and Drive Smart

When you do drive, or are driven, make the most of your trips by making multiple stops in one trip. Invite a friend to do their shopping with you. Ask your parents or guardian to make sure the family car is running efficiently. For example, keeping tires properly inflated can improve the gas mileage by more than 3 percent. Every gallon of gas saved not only saves money, but it also keeps twenty pounds of carbon dioxide out of the atmosphere.

If possible use other means of transportation. Less driving means fewer emissions. Besides saving gasoline, walking and biking are great forms of exercise. Explore your community's mass transit system, and check out options for carpooling to work or school.

5. Buy Energy-Efficient Products

Talk to your parents about home appliances that now come in a range of energy-efficient models.

Avoid products that come with excess packaging, especially molded plastic and other packaging that can't be recycled. If you reduce your household garbage by 10 percent, you can save 1,200 pounds of carbon dioxide annually.

6. Take reusable cloth bags for grocery shopping

7. Use the Off Switch

Save electricity by turning off lights when you leave a room, and using only as much light as you need. And remember to turn off your television, video player, stereo, and computer when you're not using them. Some appliances and devices draw power even when they're turned off. Obtain a smart power strip that completely turns off the power to your electronics to save electricity.

8. Turn Off the Water When You're Not Using it

While brushing your teeth, shampooing the dog, or doing chores, turn off the water until you actually need it for rinsing. You'll reduce the water bill and help to conserve a vital resource. Ask your parents to install a faucet with a motion sensor.

9. Use Cardboard boxes in your home to collect recyclables

Reserve one box for newspapers; another for batteries, glass, cans, and plastic bottles; and a third for mixed paper (cereal boxes, cardboard, envelopes, white paper, catalogs, etc.).

10. Encourage Others to Conserve

Share information about recycling and energy conservation with your friends, neighbors, and coworkers, and take opportunities to encourage public officials to establish programs and policies that are good for the environment.

Crafty Girl

Items that you may have thought had no more use can provide you with the parts for unique craft designs.

After reading this section you'll be able to turn milk into plastic, make a simple calculator with a cup, produce sneaky greeting cards, make a paper banger noisemaker, and more.

After you create your sneaky crafts, be sure to show them to family, friends, and school mates. You'll inspire them to rethink what they intended to throw away and reuse items in unintended ways (and save useful items a trip to the landfill).

Sneaky Pencil Spinner

Pencils are great for writing letters and drawing illustrations. But with a little work, you can transform one into a hand-powered fan and demonstrate the principle of energy conversion.

What's Needed
▶ Pencil with eraser
▶ Scissors
▶ Paper
▶ Straight pin with flat head
▶ Coffee stirrer or straw

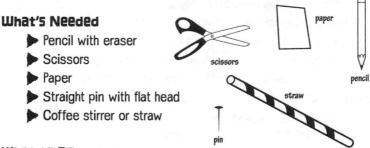

scissors

paper

pencil

straw

pin

What to Do
Carefully use one blade of the scissors to cut seven V-shaped notches in the pencil, as shown in **Figure 1**.

Then, cut a piece of paper into a 3 by 1-inch rectangle. Poke a hole in the center of the paper and stick it into the center of the pencil eraser. See **Figures 2** and **3**.

Last, hold the pencil horizontally and rub the stirrer back and forth across the pencil notches. You'll soon see the paper spin. The rubbing motion across the pencil ridges are transferred to the paper fan, causing it to rotate as shown, in **Figure 4**.

If, desired, draw a spiral design on the paper for a nice visual effect.

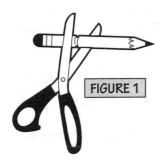

FIGURE 1

FIGURE 2

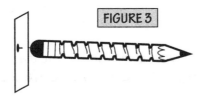

FIGURE 3

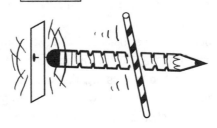

FIGURE 4

Paper Banger

This popular project has been around for ages. By folding a piece of paper in a particular pattern, you can capture enough air to cause an extremely loud popping sound.

Just follow the simple steps below and you'll be able to create this paper banger anytime.

What's Needed

▶ Letter-size (8½ by 11-inch) sheet of paper

paper

What to Do

First, fold the left and right sides of the paper toward the center and then unfold them, as shown in **Figure 1**. Next, fold all four corners toward the centerline. See **Figure 2**.

Then, fold the paper toward you, as shown in **Figure 3**, and ensure that it encloses the flaps. Fold down the banger's right side to the bottom. See **Figure 4**. Fold down the left side to the bottom, as shown in **Figure 5**.

Bend the paper back until the two points face toward you and the banger appears to have a triangular shape. See **Figure 6**. Now hold the top two corners together with your fingers and swing the banger down quickly. This will cause air to gather and compress inside the pocket to create a loud bang. See **Figure 7**.

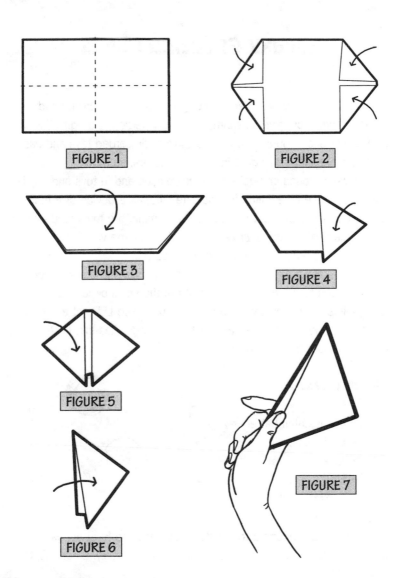

FIGURE 1

FIGURE 2

FIGURE 3

FIGURE 4

FIGURE 5

FIGURE 6

FIGURE 7

Sneaky Greeting Cards

To make an impression on someone, give a gift. For a unique and lasting impression, give a handmade sneaky personalized gift. This project will show you how to use parts from discarded toys and gadgets to make electronic greeting cards, posters, and more.

LEDs are found in most electronic devices and in toys and appliances. They are little lights that indicate whether a device or a function is on. Unlike ordinary lightbulbs, these miniature marvels do not have a filament, produce virtually no heat, consume very little power, and (when properly powered) never burn out!

You can obtain LEDs from old discarded toys and other devices. You will need to cut their leads away from the small circuit board, using pliers or wire cutters. You can also purchase LEDs at electronic parts stores locally. You can also obtain blinking LEDs that flash on and off without requiring other components.

What's Needed

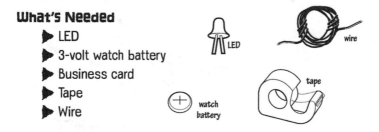

- ▶ LED
- ▶ 3-volt watch battery
- ▶ Business card
- ▶ Tape
- ▶ Wire

What to Do

Since LEDs require 2 to 5 volts to operate, the best compact power supply for them is a 3-volt lithium watch battery. Since AA, C, and D cell batteries provide just 1½ volts each, you would need two cells to provide 3 volts (although larger cells will last longer).

To see how an LED works, press its leads on both sides of a 3-volt battery, as shown in **Figure 1.** If the LED doesn't light, reverse the battery position or reverse the LED leads.

Figure 2 shows how to make a sneaky "touch switch" with a folded business card, stiff wire, and tape. Tape the wires to the card and roll up a piece of tape to act as a spacer. When properly positioned, a slight press of the folded card will connect the wires and light the LED.

LEDs can be mounted on greeting cards and bookmarks, belts and bracelets, behind posters, on trophies—and even on clothing! They can add value to items you might otherwise throw away.

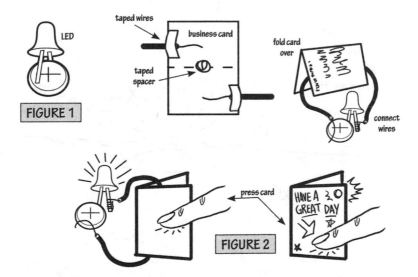

LED

FIGURE 1

taped wires

business card

fold card over

taped spacer

connect wires

press card

HAVE A GREAT DAY

FIGURE 2

Milk into Plastic

Have you ever needed plastic molding material for a repair or a craft project? Perhaps you broke off a plastic piece from a toy or an appliance and need to fill in the unsightly gap. Well, you can transform commonplace items in your kitchen into a flexible compound that will do such repairs and even allow you to paint to match.

Believe it or not, you can make a malleable plastic material from plain household milk and only one other ingredient—vinegar. It's easy.

What's Needed

- Milk
- Small pot
- Spoon
- Vinegar
- Strainer
- Jar
- Paper towels

paper towel

vinegar

milk

FIGURE 1

don't boil!

What to Do

Pour an 8-ounce cup of milk in a pot and heat it on a stove. Let it warm but not boil. Add a tablespoon of vinegar and stir the mixture. Soon, clumps of a solid material will form on the surface. Continue stirring (see **Figure 1**).

Place the strainer on top of the jar and pour the mixture through the strainer. Use the spoon to press the clumps and squeeze out the liquid, which is discarded. Remove the material from the strainer and place it on a paper towel. Dab paper towels on top of the material to absorb excess moisture (see **Figure 2**).

The solid material that has formed is called casein. It separates from milk when an acid, like vinegar, is added. Casein is used in industry to make glue, paint, and some plastics. You can now form the "sneaky plastic" into shape with a mold or use your hands. Allow the shaped material to dry for 1 to 2 days.

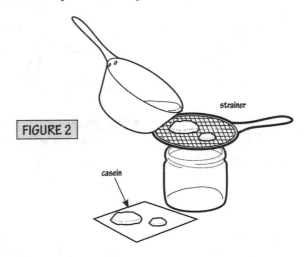

FIGURE 2

strainer

casein

Sneaky plastic has many uses. First, it allows you to recycle spoiled milk that would be discarded anyway. You can make impressions of coins and other small objects. You can shape the plastic into parts to replace items such as broken Walkman belt clips. Or you can make a personalized key ring ornament (see **Figure 3**).

Here are some more ideas for putting this plastic compound to use:

Child-proofing items with sharp edges or points
Toy assembly aid (to hold wood and plastic pieces together)
Caulk for small holes in a boat
Pendant holder
Wheels for carts and toys
Tool handle
Material for a spacer or washer
Guitar pick
Bottle cap
Temporary plumbing repairs
Waterproof container
Fishing lure and float
Replacement button

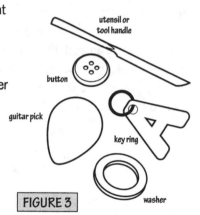

utensil or tool handle

button

guitar pick

key ring

washer

FIGURE 3

Whether you use the compound for critical repairs or just for fun craft projects, you'll discover it provides plenty of versatility with only a small investment of time.

Sneaky Balancing Tricks

You can make everyday things balance in sneaky ways when you know the secret to determining the center of gravity. The center of gravity is the point in an object at which its mass is in equilibrium. Where this point is depends on the object's shape and weight distribution, and you can produce some attention-getting creations with this knowledge.

The following four projects are easy to do with items found just about everywhere.

Sneaky Balancer I

Knowing how to lower the center of gravity of an object allows you to produce figures that seemingly defy gravity (or make you seem like a skilled magician). This project demonstrates what happens when two similar cardboard figures have their center of gravity in different positions.

What's Needed
▶ Scissors
▶ Cardboard, a piece 8½ by 11 inches

Optional:
▶ Sewing thread

scissors

sewing thread

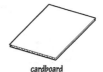
cardboard

What to Do

Cut out the small shape shown in **Figure 1** from the piece of cardboard. Follow the dimensions shown. Next, try to balance the head of the figure on your fingertip, as shown in **Figure 2**. It's almost impossible to keep it upright without its tipping over.

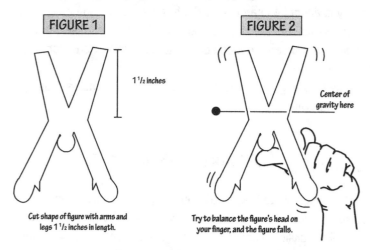

FIGURE 1

1 ¹/₂ inches

Cut shape of figure with arms and legs 1 ¹/₂ inches in length.

FIGURE 2

Center of gravity here

Try to balance the figure's head on your finger, and the figure falls.

Next, cut out the figure shown in **Figure 3**. The only difference is the legs are much longer. Try to balance this larger figure on your hand. It's easy now, because the center of gravity is below your finger. See **Figure 4**. You should be able to walk around the room and the figure will not fall.

Going Further

To demonstrate how acrobats keep their balance, cut a small slit in the head of the figure. See **Figure 5**.

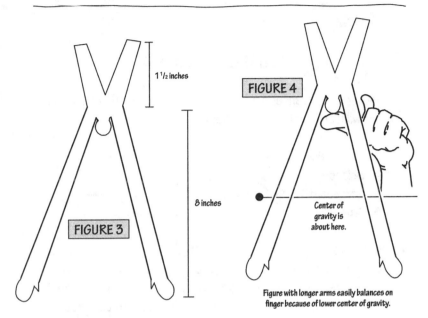

1 1/2 inches

FIGURE 4

8 inches

FIGURE 3

Center of
gravity is
about here.

Figure with longer arms easily balances on
finger because of lower center of gravity.

Then, tie a length of thread from a chair to a lower object, such
as another chair or table, and set the figure on the thread. The figure
should rest on the thread in its slit and, with a slight push, slide
across without falling. See **Figure 6**.

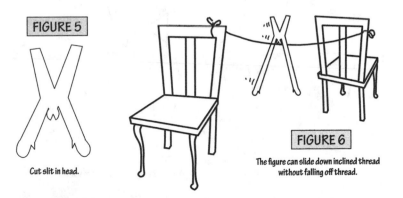

FIGURE 5

Cut slit in head.

FIGURE 6

The figure can slide down inclined thread
without falling off thread.

Sneaky Balancer II

This sneaky balancer can rest horizontally on the tip of a paper clip and will surely astonish onlookers.

What's Needed

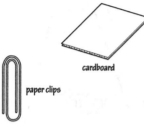

▶ Scissors
▶ Cardboard
▶ Paper clip

scissors

paper clips

cardboard

What to Do

Cut out the figure shown in **Figure 1** from the piece of cardboard. Be sure to include the spiked hair, with a long center spike. Try to adhere to the dimensions shown but, if desired, you can produce a larger or smaller figure as long as you keep the arm and body lengths in proportion.

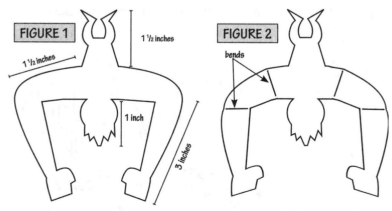

FIGURE 1

1 ½ inches

1 ½ inches

1 inch

3 inches

Cut out figure from cardboard box.

FIGURE 2

bends

Bend down the arms of the figure.

Bend the figure's arms down at the shoulder and elbows. See **Figure 2**.

Next, bend a paper clip, as shown in **Figure 3**, so one end stands up vertically.

Last, place the figure on the paper clip with the spiked hair resting on the tip. If necessary, bend the arms down so it won't fall. The figure should balance on the tip of the paper clip. You should be able to carefully push its legs to the right or left and it will stay aloft. See **Figure 4**.

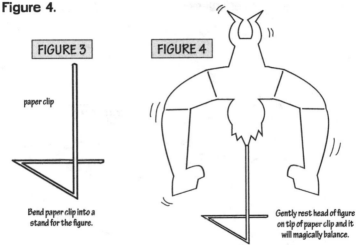

FIGURE 3

paper clip

Bend paper clip into a
stand for the figure.

FIGURE 4

Gently rest head of figure
on tip of paper clip and it
will magically balance.

Sneaky Balancer III

What's Needed

▶ Scissors
▶ Cardboard, 8½ by 11 inches

scissors

cardboard

What to Do

Cut out the shape shown in **Figure 1** from the cardboard. Be careful to follow the dimensions shown.

You should be able to easily balance the figure on the tip of your finger, elbow, or nose, because its center of gravity is at the large circular area. See **Figure 2**.

You can create similar figures and, using paper clips or coins secured with tape, add weight to an area near the bottom section of the figure so it balances effortlessly.

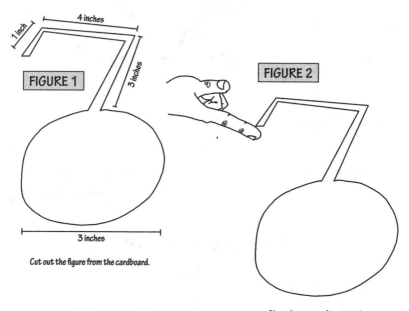

Cut out the figure from the cardboard.

Since the center of gravity is low, the figure will balance easily.

Sneaky Balancer IV

What's Needed
▶ One quarter
▶ Two metal forks
▶ Drinking cup

drinking cup

metal forks

quarter

What to Do

Place the quarter between the teeth of the two forks as shown in **Figure 1**.

If a lightweight cup is used, you must fill it with water so it will not tip over. If a heavy cup or jar is used, water is not required.

Carefully rest the quarter on the lip of the cup. You should be able to let go and the forks will stay aloft. If they don't, adjust the angle of the forks until they balance. See **Figure 2**.

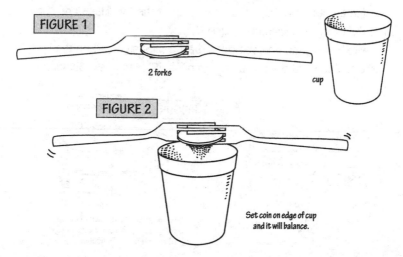

FIGURE 1

2 forks

cup

FIGURE 2

Set coin on edge of cup
and it will balance.

Sneaky Calculator

You can create a simple-to-make toy for young children just learning addition and subtraction. You just need a couple of discarded Styrofoam cups and a pen. Plus, you'll prevent the cups from needlessly filling up landfill space.

What's Needed

styrofoam cups

pen

ruler

▶ Two white, rimmed Styrofoam cups

▶ Pen

▶ Ruler

What to Do

First, obtain two cups that have a lip at the top. Place one cup into the other as shown in **Figure 1**.

Next, using the pen and ruler, draw a plus sign (+) on the lip of the top cup and the numbers 1 through 20 exactly ¼ inch apart.

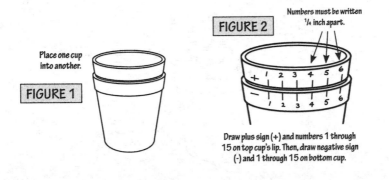

Place one cup into another.

FIGURE 1

FIGURE 2

Numbers must be written ¼ inch apart.

Draw plus sign (+) and numbers 1 through 15 on top cup's lip. Then, draw negative sign (-) and 1 through 15 on bottom cup.

Similarly, draw a negative sign (−) on the rim of the bottom cup and the numbers 1 through 20 exactly ¼ inch apart. See **Figure 2**.

HOW to Add Numbers

Following the arrows in the example shown in **Figure 3**, start with a number on the bottom cup, in this case the number 5. Turn the top cup so the plus sign (+) is above the number 5 on the bottom cup. Then, select a number on the top cup that you want to add to 5. In this instance, it is the number 3. Look at the number below 3, on the bottom cup, and the answer is 8.

You can repeat this process with any number adding up to 20. Select a number on the lower cup, align the plus sign above it, and then on the top cup select a number to add. You will see the sum immediately below the number you added.

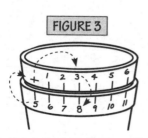

To add, start with bottom cup's number; match with (+) on top cup and number to add. The sum is below that number on the lower cup. Example: 5 (+) 3 = 8

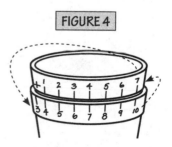

To subtract, select a number on the bottom cup, in this example 10. Align it with the number to subtract, which is 7. The answer is below the (+) sign: 3.

How to Subtract Numbers

See the example problem in **Figure 4** and follow the arrows. Start with a number on the bottom cup, in this case the number 10. Turn the top cup so the number you wish to subtract is above the first number you selected on the bottom cup. In this instance it is the number 7. Then, look at the plus sign (+) on the top cup. Below the symbol, on the bottom cup, is the answer: the number 3.

You can repeat this process with any number up to 20. Select a number on the lower cup and turn the cup to align it with the number on the top cup that you wish to subtract. Look at the plus sign on the top cup and you'll see the answer below it on the lower cup.

Sneaky Puzzles

Working with puzzles can be fun. But some puzzles are expensive and/or complicated, and must be worked on at home.

This project will illustrate how to make portable picture puzzles. By using pictures from discarded greeting cards and magazines, you'll be able to create unique puzzles using your favorite pictures from today's headlines.

What's Needed

- ▶ Pictures from popular magazines or greeting cards
- ▶ Scissors
- ▶ Glue
- ▶ Cardboard from a food container, such as a cereal box
- ▶ Velcro dots with sticky tape backing

magazine

scissors

glue

small
cardboard box

Optional

- ▶ Small magnets with sticky backs

What to Do

Select and cut out a picture from a magazine and glue it to a piece of cardboard. After the glue has dried, cut the picture into smaller pieces. See **Figure 1**.

Next, apply Velcro dots to the bottom pieces of the pictures. Also stick Velcro dots to another piece of cardboard, as shown in **Figure 2**. Now you have a simple puzzle you can play with anytime and anywhere, even upside down. See **Figure 3**.

Since the puzzle pieces have Velcro dots attached, they can be placed elsewhere than the cardboard. With matching Velcro dots applied to the inside of lockers, cabinets, a favorite bag, or articles of clothing, you can play your puzzles anywhere you desire, as shown in **Figure 4**.

Your sneaky puzzle pictures also can be made using small magnets with sticky back surfaces, allowing you to place your puzzles on refrigerator doors and other steel surfaces.

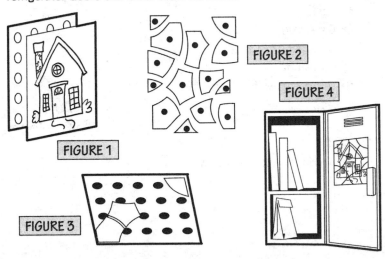

FIGURE 1

FIGURE 2

FIGURE 3

FIGURE 4

Sneaky Bubble Maker

Here's a neat way to make your own bubbles anytime you wish. By using some easily found items from the kitchen, you'll save yourself the time and expense of purchasing a bubble-making kit from the store (and save our valuable resources).

What's Needed
▶ Twist ties or paper clips
▶ Dishwashing liquid
▶ Cup or bowl
▶ Water

water

bowl

detergent

paper clips

What to Do
Bend a twist tie into a loop shape. Then, bend a second twist tie around the first one to act as a handle, as shown in **Figure 1**. You can also bend two paper clips into a larger loop and handle, if desired.

FIGURE 1

FIGURE 2

Next, pour ½ teaspoon of dishwashing liquid into a glass or small bowl and fill it with water. Stir the water slowly to mix the liquids but not too fast, as that creates bubbles too soon. See **Figure 2**.

Last, dip the twist-tie loop into the solution and lift it upward carefully until you have a cohesive layer of fluid covering the loop. Then blow the solution into a large bubble, as shown in **Figure 3**.

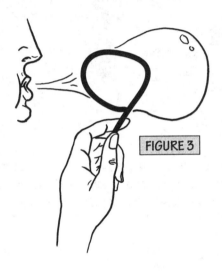

FIGURE 3

CD Showcase

Empty CD cases can be used as one of the rare make-it-yourself gifts for holidays and birthdays that look great yet will not cost a thing.

Here's a way to make an attractive showcase for your favorite photos and prevent plastic from unnecessarily filling our landfills at the same time.

What's Needed

- Empty CD case
- Photograph
- Construction or wrapping paper
- Glue
- Scissors

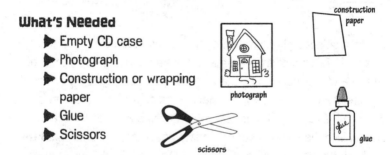

construction paper

photograph

scissors

glue

What to Do

First, cut two pieces of paper the same size as a typical CD label, which are generally 4¾ inches square, as shown in **Figure 1**.

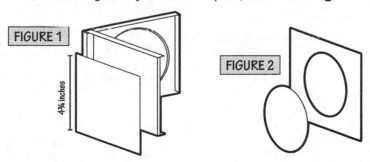

FIGURE 1

4¾ inches

FIGURE 2

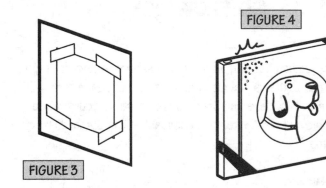

FIGURE 4

FIGURE 3

Next, select a photograph for showcasing in the CD frame and measure it. Cut a hole slightly smaller than the photo in the center of one piece of the paper, to create a mat frame. See **Figure 2**.

Then, tape or glue the photo behind the paper so you can see it through the opening. If desired, you can place a second piece of paper behind the photograph for a neat appearance, as shown in **Figure 3**. Fit the framed photo inside the CD case to serve as its cover.

You can decorate the CD showcase further with ribbons, sparkles, and other craft pieces, as you desire. See **Figure 4**.

Write Stuff

We all use pens and pencils and usually don't give them a second thought. But you can easily decorate and accessorize your writing tools with everyday items.

By following these directions, your sneaky pens won't be limited to a single design. At any time, you'll be able to attach extra accessories when the mood strikes.

What's Needed
- Fabric
- Pen
- Scissors
- Glue
- Velcro strips with sticky tape backing
- Small magnets
- Paper clips

scissors

velcro

glue

small magnets

paper clips

Optional:
- Felt
- Additional fabric
- Small plastic pieces
- Small pictures

pen

pictures

What to Do

Wrap a piece of fabric around your pen and cut it so it's slightly larger than the pen. To hold the fabric on the pen, you can either glue it in place or apply two small Velcro strips to each end of the pen, as shown in **Figure 1**, applying Velcro strips to the fabric and wrapping it around the pen. See **Figure 2**. You can decorate the pen with felt, more fabric, and small plastic pieces glued to the fabric, as desired.

Optionally, you can glue or Velcro small magnets to the pen before it's covered, this allows steel objects, such as paper clips, to be attached to and removed from the pen as desired. See the small picture holder example in **Figure 3**.

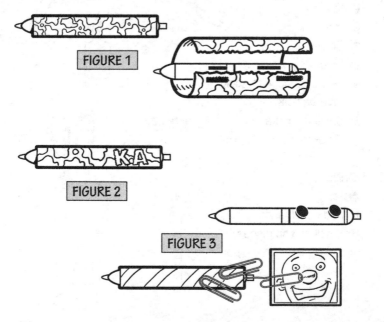

FIGURE 1

FIGURE 2

FIGURE 3

Color-Change Disc Spinner

Challenge your friends by asking them to change the color of an item without touching or painting it. Then amaze your friends when you actually produce colors from a black-and-white image with this next trick.

What's Needed
▶ White cardboard
▶ Black marker
▶ Pencil
▶ Pin
▶ Scissors

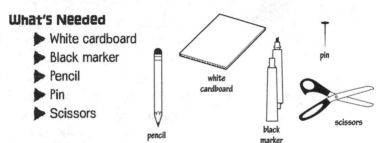

pencil

white cardboard

black marker

pin

scissors

What to Do
Draw the disc shown in **Figure 1** on the white cardboard. Ensure that half the disc is solid black and half has the broken circle picture. If you photocopy the illustration, be sure to fill in blank spots with a marker. The disc should be approximately 4 inches in diameter. Cut out the disc with the scissors.

Place the disc on the center of the pencil eraser. Secure the disc to the eraser by pushing the pin into the eraser through the cardboard. See **Figure 2**.

Next, place the pencil between your palms and spin it. You'll see the black-and-white image turn blue and red depending on the speed, as shown in **Figure 3**.

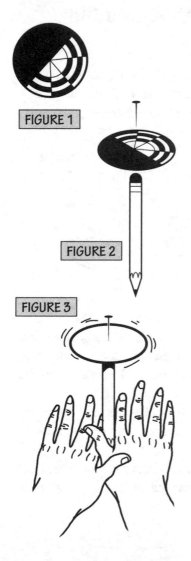

FIGURE 1

FIGURE 2

FIGURE 3

How It Works

Your eyes have rod cells for peripheral, or side, vision, and cone cells for front vision and for discerning color.

There are three different types of cone cells that each respond to red, green, and blue at different response times. When you see white, all three cone cells respond equally. When you spin the disc, the alternating black sections, with their different lengths, cause an imbalance to how the three cone cells respond to white and your cone cells cause you to "see" different colors.

Sneaky Bracelet, Purse, Sneakers, and Hat Accessories

With easily found items, you can personalize your jewelry, handbags, and footwear. The best thing is that, with sneaky design techniques, your accessories become adaptable, allowing you to mix and match your new creations according to your mood.

What's Needed

- Velcro strips or dots with sticky tape backing
- Small, strong magnets
- Plastic
- Fabric
- Flexible flashlight
- LED blinkers
- Personal alarm

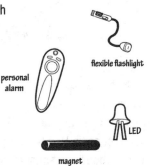

personal alarm

flexible flashlight

LED

magnet

What to Do

By applying Velcro dots or strips on your sneakers, you can add your initials, symbols, logos, and artwork made of spare plastic and fabric. See **Figure 1**.

FIGURE 1

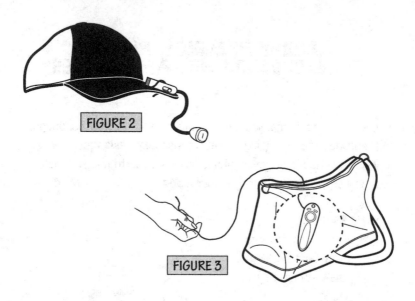

FIGURE 2

FIGURE 3

It's easy to add a clip-on flexible flashlight to your favorite cap, as shown in **Figure 2**.

By placing small, strong magnets in your bracelets, caps, and handbags, you can apply LED blinking lights for a unique touch.

If you desire, add a personal alarm to your handbag so when you sit it down, the alarm will sound if someone attempts to steal it, as shown in **Figure 3**.

Making Hand Shadows

Most of us are amazed when we see people make lifelike shadows using just their hands. With just a light source and a wall, you can show off some sneaky shadows with a little practice.

The sneaky trick is to form a shape with each hand individually and join them. Look at the shadow figures and follow the directions for each hand as you watch the figure appear. You'll quickly memorize many interesting figures and develop more on your own.

Start with the following hand-shadow shapes below:

Deer

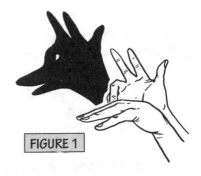

FIGURE 1

Left hand: Curl your thumb in your palm and tilt all of your fingers slightly downward. Leave a little gap between your little and fourth fingers for the mouth.

Right hand: With your hand behind your left hand, hold up your middle and index fingers and thumb until the shadow resembles the deer's head and ears. See **Figure 1**.

Elephant

Left hand: Hold your hand and fingers straight out with your little finger slightly separated. Allow the thumb, middle, and index fingers to droop down to form the trunk and mouth.

Right hand: Position the hand above the left hand with the fingers curved, as shown in **Figure 2**.

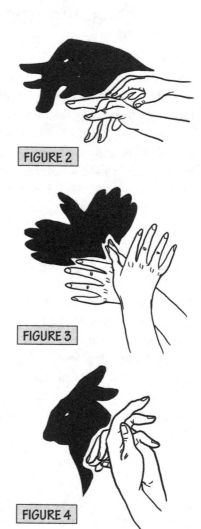

FIGURE 2

Bird

Hold up and spread your left and right hands with the thumbs pressed together. Curl and spread the fingers to simulate the wings flapping. See **Figure 3**.

FIGURE 3

Rabbit

Right hand: Hold the hand and fingers in an unclenched fist shape.

Left hand: Hold the hand upright with the forefinger and thumb almost straight up, the middle finger at a right angle and the ring finger pointing down. See **Figure 4**.

FIGURE 4

Dog Head

Right hand: Hold the hand and thumb straight up. Point the little and ring fingers straight out horizontally. Point the index finger and middle finger downward, as shown in **Figure 5**.

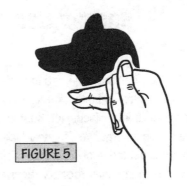

FIGURE 5

Boy

Right hand: Position your hand as if you are grabbing the handle of a mug.

Left hand: Place your hand above the left hand in a clawing shape as if you are about to grab something. See **Figure 6**.

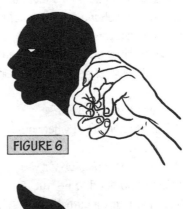

FIGURE 6

Goose

Right hand: Hold your hand at a 45-degree angle with the ring and little fingers extended. Bend the thumb. Curve the index finger and bend the middle finger beneath it. See **Figure 7**.

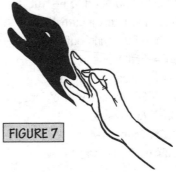

FIGURE 7

Sneaky Cell Phone Tricks

With the popularity and rise in use of real-time text-based communications, such as instant messaging, e-mail, Internet, and online gaming chat rooms, discussion boards, and cell phone text messaging, came the emergence of a new language tailored to the immediacy and compactness of these new communication media. If you have ever been in a chat room or received an instant message or text message from someone that seemed to be in its own foreign language, the Webopedia Quick Reference (www.webopedia.com/quick-ref) will help you decipher the text chat lingo, providing the definitions to seven hundred frequently used chat abbreviations. Some of the most popular terms are listed below:

? I have a question

? I don't understand what you mean

?4U I have a question for you

2G2BT Too good to be true

2MI Too much information

4COL For crying out loud

4EAE Forever and ever

AAK Asleep at keyboard

AAMOF As a matter of fact

AAR At any rate

ACK Acknowledge

AFAIK As far as I know

AFC Away from computer

AFK Away from keyboard

AIGHT All right

B4N Bye for now

BAG Busting a gut

BAK Back at keyboard

BBIAF Be back in a few

BBIAM Be back in a minute

BBIAS Be back in a sec

BBL Be back later

BBN Bye, bye now

BBT Be back tomorrow

BC Because

BCNU Be seeing you

BCOS Because

BTW By the way

C&G Chuckle & grin

CB Coffee break or chat break

CRB Come right back

CYAL8R See you later

CYE Check your e-mail

CYO See you online

DKDC Don't know, don't care

DM Doesn't matter

d00d Dude

DQMOT Don't quote me on this

EMA E-mail address

EMFBI Excuse me for butting in

EMSG E-mail message

ENUF Enough

EOD End of day

F2F Face to face

F2T Free to talk

FWIW For what it's worth

G2CU Good to see you

G2G Got to go

G2R Got to run

GJ Good job

GL Good luck

GL/HF Good luck, have fun

HAU How about you?

H&K Hugs & kisses

H2CUS Hope to see you soon

IAC In any case

IDK I don't know

IDTS I don't think so

IDUNNO I don't know

IG2R I got to run

IM Instant message

IMHO In my humble opinion

IRL In real life

IRMC I rest my case

JAC Just a sec

JAM Just a minute

JJA Just joking around

JK Just kidding

JW Just wondering

K Okay

KB or **k/b** Keyboard

KEWL Cool

KIT Keep in touch

L8R Later

LD Later, dude

LOL Laughing out loud

LQTM Laughing quietly to myself

LTS Laughing to self

MNC Mother nature calls

MTF More to follow

N1 Nice one

NBD No big deal
OB Oh brother
OIC Oh, I see
RL Real life
RLY Really
ROFL Rolling on floor laughing
SAL Such a laugh
SC Stay cool
SH Same here
SIG2R Sorry, I got to run
SRSLY Seriously
SS So sorry
ST&D Stop texting and drive
SUP What's up?
T+ Think positive
TA Thanks a lot
TAFN That's all for now
TBC To be continued
TIAD Tomorrow is another day
TIC Tongue-in-cheek
TLK2UL8R Talk to you later
TMB Text me back
TMI Too much information
TTYL Talk to you later
TTYS Talk to you soon

UGTBK You've got to be kidding
URTM You are the man
UV Unpleasant visual
UW You're welcome
VM Voice mail
VN Very nice
WAM Wait a minute
WAN2TLK Want to talk
WB Welcome back
WBS Write back soon
WDYK What do you know?
WDYT What do you think?
WWNC Will wonders never cease
WWYC Write when you can
WYD What (are) you doing?
YCMU You crack me up
YSYD Yeah sure you do
YT You there?
YTG You're the greatest
YW You're welcome
ZOT Zero tolerance
ZUP What's up?
ZZ's are calling (going to bed)
ZZZZ Sleeping (or bored)

Smiley Faces: Showing Sneaky Emotions

Use your keyboard characters and punctuation to create a sideways face:

▶ The colon and close parenthesis represents a
   sideways smile :)
▶ Use a hyphen to add a nose :-)
▶ Use a semicolon and a close parenthesis to make a
   winking face ;)
▶ Add a dash for a nose ;-)

Here are some variations, also from Webopedia:

:) Standard smile   :-# With braces
:-) Standard smile with nose   :'-) Happy crying
:-E Buck-tooth   ;) Winking smile
: (Sad smile   ;-) Winking smile with nose
:-(Sad with nose   :-D Laughter
:-< Super sad |-O Yawning
: P Sticking tongue out   :@) Pig smile

Magic Girl

Here are some fun and foolproof tricks you can do anytime to amaze your friends. Each sneaky trick uses odds and ends you have with you or around the house. The best part? These illusions don't require a big production, special skills, or dexterity.

Want to know how to spin paper with your hands without touching it, turn a black-and-white image into color, step through a postcard, tie a knot with one hand, and other sneaky magic tricks? They're all here.

With a little preparation and your personalized delivery, you'll be ready at a moment's notice to perform some amazing feats.

Before you rush and show off your new tricks, be sure to follow the sneaky magician's rules:

- Practice until you can do the sneaky trick with your eyes closed.
- Don't reveal the secret behind the trick.
- Don't repeat an illusion to the same audience.

Paper Magic

Paper folding is fun but you can enhance your enjoyment by making the following sneaky origami designs that include motion action using everyday things.

Sneaky Head-Bobbing Bird

What's Needed

▶ Scissors
▶ Paper
▶ Pencil

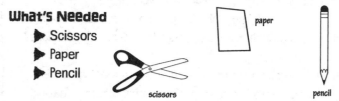

paper

scissors

pencil

What to Do

Cut the paper into a square and fold/unfold both the diagonals, as shown in **Figure 1**. Fold over the top left and right corners to the center. See **Figure 2**.

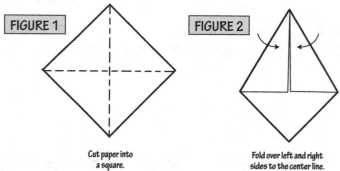

FIGURE 1

Cut paper into
a square.

FIGURE 2

Fold over left and right
sides to the center line.

Then, fold over the lower left and right corners toward the center as shown in **Figure 3**. Fold up the bottom point to the center line to form a tail and fold the top corner toward the back of the figure to make the head, as shown in **Figures 4** and **5**.

Next, fold the figure in half vertically along the center toward the tail. This will bend the tail and head outward as shown in **Figure 6**. Draw eyes and a beak on the figure as desired.

Last, with the sneaky bird standing upright, push down on the center of the tail. The head should move downward. See **Figure 7**.

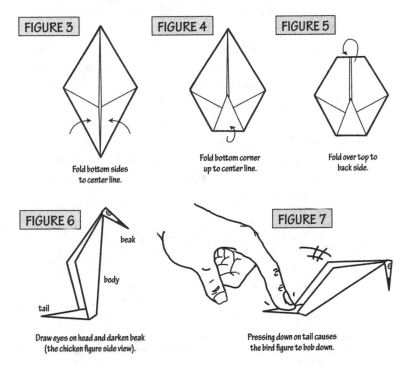

FIGURE 3
Fold bottom sides
to center line.

FIGURE 4
Fold bottom corner
up to center line.

FIGURE 5
Fold over top to
back side.

FIGURE 6
beak
body
tail
Draw eyes on head and darken beak
(the chicken figure side view).

FIGURE 7
Pressing down on tail causes
the bird figure to bob down.

Sneaky Mouth Flapper

What's Needed

▶ Scissors
▶ Paper
▶ Pencil

pencil

paper

scissors

What to Do

Cut the paper into a square, as shown in **Figure 1**. Next, fold and unfold the square on both the diagonals. Fold over the lower left and right corners to the center. See **Figure 2**.

Then, fold over the upper left and right corners toward the center, as shown in **Figure 3**. Fold up the bottom half of the figure along the center crease. See **Figure 4**. Fold down the top front corner to the bottom of the figure, as shown in **Figure 5**.

Fold the top back tip down and to the left along the fold line shown in **Figure 5**. Then, fold the bottom front tip up and to the left along its indicated diagonal fold line, until it resembles the shape in **Figure 6**. Unfold the left-pointing tips back to their positions shown in **Figure 5**. See **Figure 7**.

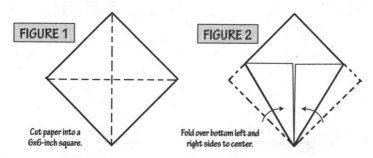

FIGURE 1

Cut paper into a
6x6-inch square.

FIGURE 2

Fold over bottom left and
right sides to center.

Next, fold the top corner down and to the right in the opposite direction of how you folded it to make **Figure 6**. Similarly, fold the bottom corner up but to the right, until the shape appears like the one in **Figure 8**.

Fold the bottom right corner to the center—it will fold the figure in half. See **Figure 9**. While you are folding it, shape the top right-pointing corners into a mouth shape by pushing the beak with your hand. See **Figure 10**. If necessary, fold and unfold the figure until this section resembles a mouth.

Last, draw eyes on both sides of the top portion of the figure. Now you can pull on the two bottom corners and the mouth will flap open and closed, as shown in **Figure 11**. If not, unfold the beak and refold it while adjusting it with your hand until the mouth moves properly.

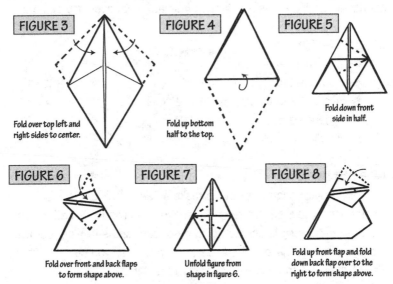

FIGURE 3

Fold over top left and right sides to center.

FIGURE 4

Fold up bottom half to the top.

FIGURE 5

Fold down front side in half.

FIGURE 6

Fold over front and back flaps to form shape above.

FIGURE 7

Unfold figure from shape in figure 6.

FIGURE 8

Fold up front flap and fold down back flap over to the right to form shape above.

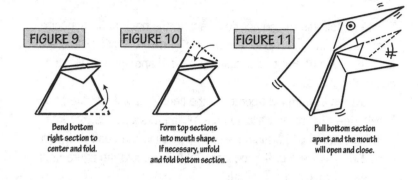

FIGURE 9

Bend bottom
right section to
center and fold.

FIGURE 10

Form top sections
into mouth shape.
If necessary, unfold
and fold bottom section.

FIGURE 11

Pull bottom section
apart and the mouth
will open and close.

Sneaky Origami Animator

You can add motion to your origami designs, and other craft creations, by making a Sneaky Origami Animator with everyday objects.

What's Needed

- Two large paper clips
- Electrical tape
- Five by three-inch piece of cardboard
- Needle-nose pliers

pliers

paper clips

electrical tape

cardboard

What to Do

This project illustrates how to make a cam-crank toy to add locomotion to your still figure designs. You can produce variations on this design by using larger pieces of cardboard and stiff wire, but it's recommended to make a simple version first. Later, you can alter the size of the parts to produce your desired results.

First, bend one paper clip into the shape shown in **Figure 1**. It will act as a mount for your origami figure.

Next, bend the second paper clip into the shape shown in **Figure 2**. It will act as a cranking cam that will move the first paper clip up and down. Wrap electrical tape around both paper clips.

Poke holes in the cardboard at 1-inch, 2½-inch, and 4-inch intervals, as shown in **Figure 3**. Then, stand the card along its long side and fold it into a U shape.

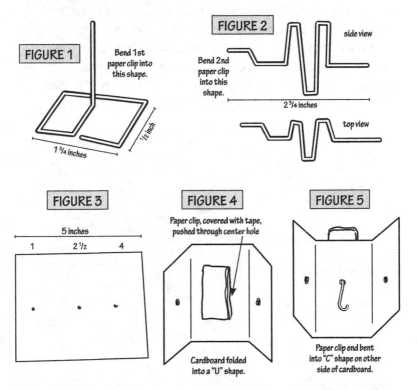

FIGURE 1 — Bend 1st paper clip into this shape. 1¾ inches, ½ inch

FIGURE 2 — Bend 2nd paper clip into this shape. side view. 2¾ inches. top view

FIGURE 3 — 5 inches. 1 2½ 4

FIGURE 4 — Paper clip, covered with tape, pushed through center hole. Cardboard folded into a "U" shape.

FIGURE 5 — Paper clip end bent into "C" shape on other side of cardboard.

Push the first paper clip into the center hole. Use pliers to bend the top of the clip into a **C** shape so it will not fall through the hole. See **Figures 4** and **5**.

Next, push the second paper clip into the side holes of the cardboard so it rests underneath the first paper clip, as shown in **Figure 6**. Apply tape to the bottom of the cardboard to keep its shape.

Last, turn the paper clip crank on the side of the Sneaky Origami Animator and the top paper clip will move up and down. See **Figure 7**. Since the first paper clip has an irregular shape, it acts as a cam mechanism and causes erratic movement on the other paper clip resting on it.

You can attach small paper figures to the top paper clip with tape. Experiment with an assortment of shapes for your paper clip cam (e.g., oval or triangular shapes) to produce a variety of motion effects. See the moving-arm figure in **Figure 8**.

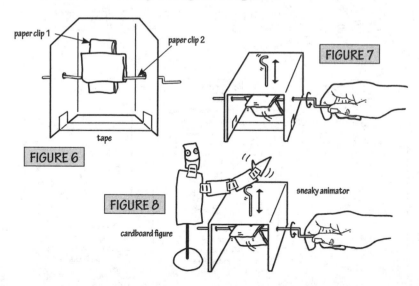

Sneaky Solonoid

When electricity flows through a wire, it produces a magnetic field around it. If a magnet is brought near the wire, it will cause the wire to move toward it (or away, depending on its position). This project shows how to use this principle to create a Sneaky Solonoid— a mechanical switch activated by a magnetic coil, commonly used to open and close an electric circuit, a lock, or a valve.

What's Needed

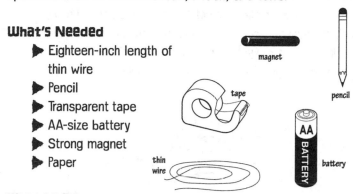

- Eighteen-inch length of thin wire
- Pencil
- Transparent tape
- AA-size battery
- Strong magnet
- Paper

magnet

pencil

tape

AA BATTERY battery

thin wire

What to Do

Strip the ends from the wire and wrap it ten turns around a pencil, using the center of the wire length to begin wrapping so that both ends are free. See **Figure 1**. Apply a small piece of tape to the wire coil to retain its shape, as shown in **Figure 2**.

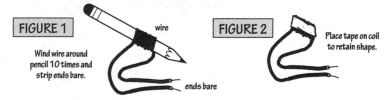

FIGURE 1   wire

Wind wire around pencil 10 times and strip ends bare.

ends bare

FIGURE 2   Place tape on coil to retain shape.

Tape one end of the wire to the AA battery's positive terminal and the other end to the side of the battery near the negative terminal. See **Figure 3**.

Place a magnet on the table and position the coil directly over it. When you press the wire on the battery's negative terminal, the wire coil will jump. If it moves toward the magnet, turn the magnet over. See **Figure 4**. *Caution: Only press the wire on the battery briefly because it will quickly heat up.*

You've made a simple solonoid. Solonoids are used in many devices, such as an electric door lock, to allow a pushbutton to control motion or allow entry through the door. They are also used in radio control models to control the wings' ailerons and rudders for flight control.

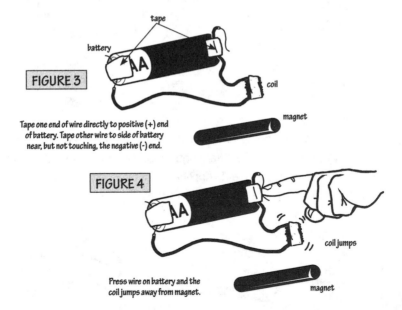

tape

battery

FIGURE 3

coil

magnet

Tape one end of wire directly to positive (+) end of battery. Tape other wire to side of battery near, but not touching, the negative (-) end.

FIGURE 4

coil jumps

Press wire on battery and the coil jumps away from magnet.

magnet

Going Further

You can make the Sneaky Solonoid animate a small origami figure by taping it to the wire coil. See **Figure 5**.

To make a simple origami beetle, follow the directions below:

Start with a 2-inch square piece of thin paper, as shown in **Figure 6A**. Fold down the top corner to the bottom corner. See **Figure 6B**. Fold over the left and right corners close, but not all the way, to the center, as shown in **Figure 6C**. **Figure 6D** shows how to fold down the top and side corners to give the origami beetle a buglike appearance. Simply tape the beetle to the wire coil and have fun making it hop and dance. *Caution: Only press the wire on the battery briefly because it will quickly heat up.*

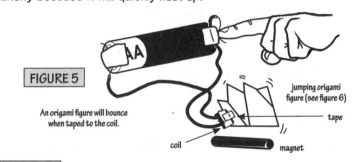

FIGURE 5

An origami figure will bounce
when taped to the coil.

jumping origami
figure (see figure 6)

tape

coil

magnet

FIGURE 6

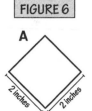

A

2 inches   2 inches

Cut a 2-inch square
piece of thin paper.

B

Fold the top corner
to the bottom.

C

Fold down the left
and right corners.

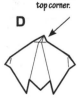

D

Bend down the
top corner.

Bend up the
side tips.

The origami "beetle" is complete.

Magic Tricks

Here are some fun and useful tricks you can do anytime to amaze your friends. The best part? Each sneaky trick uses common objects you have with you or around the house.

Make a Coin Vanish in Your Hand

Making an object disappear before the eyes of an audience is one of the most popular magic tricks. With a little practice, you'll be able to perform this simple trick anywhere with any small object.

What's Needed

 coin

▶ Coin

What to Do

Hold the coin upright in full view between your thumb and forefinger as shown in **Figure 1**.

Note: You can perform the trick in either hand. In this example, the trick begins in the left hand.

Next, place the thumb and middle finger of your right hand through the thumb and forefinger of your left hand as if you're about to grab the coin. See **Figure 2**. As you cover the coin with your fingers, and obscure its view from onlookers, let the coin drop into the palm of your left hand as shown in **Figure 3**.

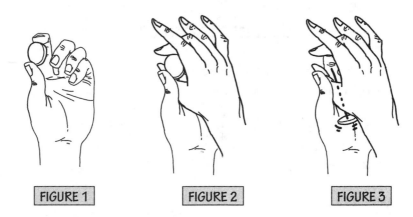

FIGURE 1   FIGURE 2   FIGURE 3

Don't immediately close your left hand. Instead, close your right hand into a fist, swing it away from your left hand, and bring it near your onlookers to bring attention to it. Show them that it's empty and point to your left hand and the coin.

To your onlookers, it appears that you grabbed the coin from your left hand and the object is in your right hand's closed fist. However, the coin was never removed from your left hand because you sneakily dropped it from your thumb and forefinger into your palm. You can also bring your left hand behind an onlooker's ear and say that you made it travel there while you open your hand to reveal the coin.

Balancing Soda Can

In this surprising trick, a soda can balances at a 45-degree angle on a surface or on your hand.

What's Needed
► Soda can
► Water

soda can

water

What to Do
First, pour out two-thirds of the soda from the can. See **Figure 1**. If you start with an empty can, pour water in it until it's one-third full.

Next, tilt the can on its edge so it stays in place as shown in **Figure 2**. If the can does not balance, add or remove liquid until the can stands on its edge.

Try balancing the can on a surface and even on your finger. For dramatic effect, act as if it takes lots of effort and skill to keep the can balanced.

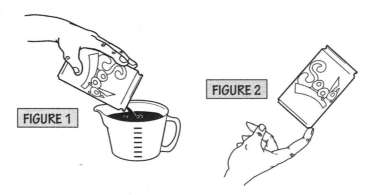

FIGURE 1

FIGURE 2

Tie a Knot With One Hand Without Letting Go Of the String

Here's a sneaky dare you can make with a friend. Challenge your friend to pick up a length of string or rope and tie a knot using only one hand. After your friend's failed attempt, you'll execute this one-handed trick. You can also perform this trick with a tightly wound scarf.

What's Needed

▶ String, rope, or scarf

rope

What to Do

First, place the string over your hand, but not your thumb, with one end hanging a few inches lower over the right side of your hand as shown in **Figure 1**.

Next, pull up the longer end using your middle and forefingers. See **Figure 2**.

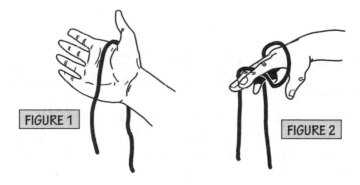

FIGURE 1

FIGURE 2

Wiggle your hand as you let the longer length of string pull through the short end, which now encircles it. Let the loop that has formed slip over the back of your hand as the long end pulls through the center. Keep wiggling your hand and soon the string will fall into a loose knot as shown in **Figure 3**.

Last, say "Presto!" and allow the string to drop down into a knot as shown in **Figure 4**.

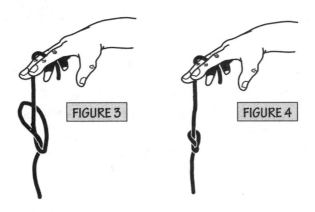

Tie a Knot With Two Hands Without Letting Go Of the String

After amazing your friend with the one-handed knot-tying trick, dare him to pick up a length of string (rope or a tightly wound scarf will also work) with the forefingers and thumbs of both hands and tie a knot without letting go.

What's Needed

▶ Two-foot length of string, rope, or a rolled up scarf

What to Do

First, place the string in front of you on a table, then cross your arms as shown in **Figure 1**.

Next, grab one end of the string with one hand and then position your arms so you can pick up the other end with your other hand. See **Figure 2**.

Last, uncross your arms and the string will magically tie a knot on its own as shown in **Figure 3**.

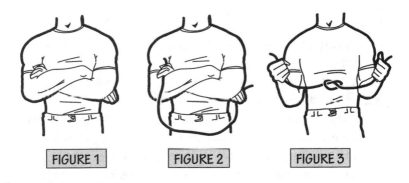

FIGURE 1   FIGURE 2   FIGURE 3

Step through a Postcard

You can win quite a few bets by performing this simple trick. Ask a friend to cut a hole in a postcard large enough to step through. Your friend can't cut strips and tape them together though.

When your friend fails to accomplish this feat, you can quickly make sneaky cuts in the postcard and amaze your onlookers.

What's Needed
▶ Postcard
▶ Scissors

postcard

scissors

What to Do

Figure 1 shows a typical postcard. Fold the postcard in half, widthwise.

Note: You can also perform this trick with a piece of paper, a business card, and so forth.

Using the scissors, cut along the lines shown in **Figure 2**. You can add more lines if desired but there must be an odd number of lines that alternate from the top and bottom of the postcard.

Next, unfold the postcard and cut across the lines shown in **Figure 3**.

Last, pull the postcard apart along the cut edges until it forms a large circular shape large enough for you to step through. See **Figure 4**.

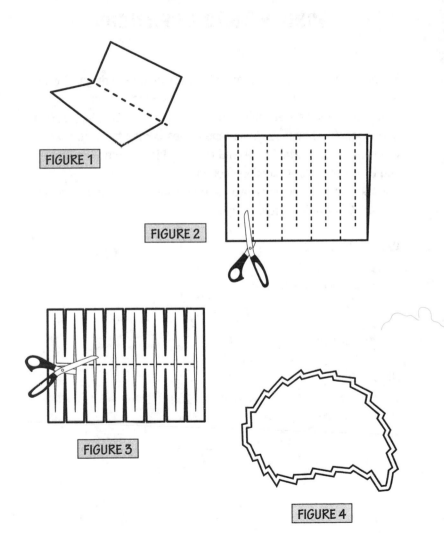

FIGURE 1

FIGURE 2

FIGURE 3

FIGURE 4

Sneaky Tape Creations

Magnetism is used to record and play back tape recordings. Tiny iron particles on recording tape align themselves according to the signal placed there by the magnetic tape recording heads. On play back, the now-magnetized material in the tape moves across the tape head, which has coils of wire inside, and the signal is detected and amplified by the recorder to produce sound.

You can make some sneaky craft designs with strips of tape and animate them with a strong magnet.

What's Needed

- Cassette tape
- Strong magnet
- Cardboard
- Glue
- Scissors

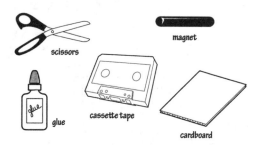

magnet

scissors

glue

cassette tape

cardboard

What to Do

First, draw a figure of your choosing. In **Figure 1**, an illustration of a man is shown.

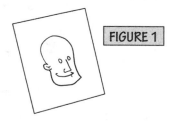

FIGURE 1

Next, cut 2- to 3-inch strips of cassette tape and place glue on one end of the tape strips. Press the strips on the figure to create hair and a beard as shown in **Figure 2**. Let the sneaky design dry for 30 minutes.

FIGURE 2

Then, bring a magnet close to the drawing near the top of the figure's head. As shown in **Figure 3**, the "hair" made from the cassette tape will stand up. Try different drawings and tape arrangements to see what other animated illustrations you can create.

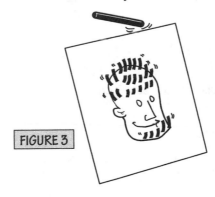

FIGURE 3

Hand-Powered Fan

As you may know, hot air rises. Rising heat can be made to move objects, and you can demonstrate this fact with a novel "hand-powered" motor. In this demonstrational science project, your hands will actually provide the heat to show how moving air currents can move an object in a rotary motion.

All it takes is an ordinary piece of paper, scissors, a needle, a cardboard box, and your hands.

What's Needed

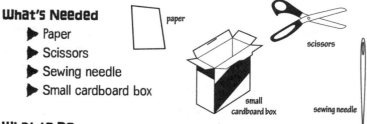

- ▶ Paper
- ▶ Scissors
- ▶ Sewing needle
- ▶ Small cardboard box

paper

scissors

small cardboard box

sewing needle

What to Do

Cut a piece of paper into a 2-inch square. Fold it in half diagonally; then unfold it and fold it in half on the other diagonal, as shown in **Figure 1.** This should create a cross-fold with a center point.

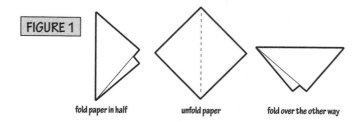

FIGURE 1

fold paper in half   unfold paper   fold over the other way

You can use a paper-clip box or similar small box as a mount for the needle. Hold the needle on its side with your fingers and carefully twist it into the top of the box (or use a thimble) until it punctures a hole in the top. Place the piece of paper on top of the needle so its center point allows the paper to turn freely. See **Figure 2**.

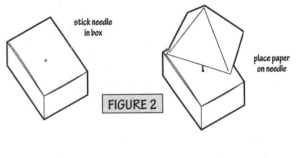

stick needle in box

place paper on needle

FIGURE 2

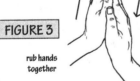

FIGURE 3

rub hands together

To make the sneaky "motor" turn, rub your hands together back and forth about twenty times to generate heat and place them near the sides of the paper. After a few seconds, the paper will begin to spin (see **Figure 3**).

The paper spins because the heat on your hands causes a temperature increase in the air around the paper. As the heated air rises and cooler air takes its place, the air movement pushes the paper sides, causing it to rotate like a motor.

place hands near paper causing it to spin

Magically Join Two Books

Ask a friend, especially a strong one, to take this simple challenge and watch the fun when he or she can't accomplish such a seemingly easy task.

What's Needed

▶ Two paperback books, similar in size

Two paperback books

What to Do

First, position the books so they face each other, as shown in **Figure 1**. Then, using your thumbs, pull up the book pages and let them fall alternately, as shown in **Figure 2**. Next, when all of the pages of both books are properly joined, slowly slide the books together as closely as you can until they overlap, as shown in **Figure 3**. Press down and rub the top book cover to remove most of the air between the pages.

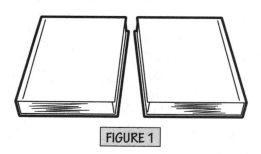

FIGURE 1

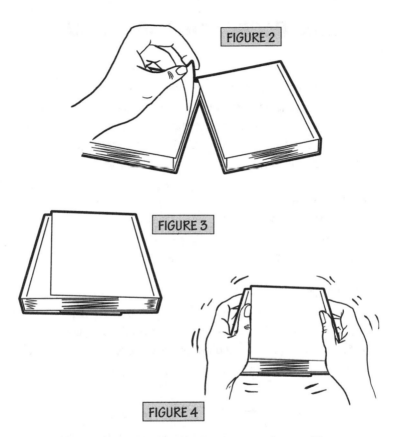

FIGURE 2

FIGURE 3

FIGURE 4

Last, ask your friend to pull the books apart for you. The person will not be able to do it. The air pressure surrounding the books and the friction make it virtually impossible to pull the books apart. See **Figure 4**.

To separate the two books, you must ruffle the pages as you slide the books apart.

Join Paper Clips on a Dollar

Some of the most interesting tricks are the ones where you use items that everyone has. Your audience is intrigued because they never thought about combining common items. Here, you can amaze your friends by telling them that you'll link two paper clips without touching them.

What's Needed

► A dollar bill or strip of paper

► Two paper clips

paper clips

What to Do

Bend the dollar bill into the loop shape shown in **Figure 1**. Next, slide the first paper clip across the top of the bill so it joins the paper. See **Figure 2**. Then, slip the other paper clip over the other end of the bill, as shown in **Figure 3**.

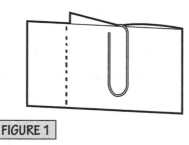

FIGURE 1

Last, say a few magic words and simply pull the two ends of the bill apart. When the paper clips detach from the bill, they will be linked together, as shown in **Figure 4**.

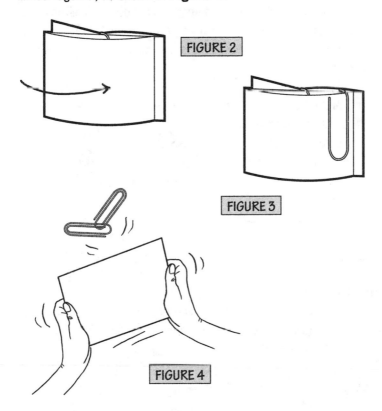

FIGURE 2

FIGURE 3

FIGURE 4

Soap-Powered Fish

When you think of cardboard and detergent, you don't usually imagine that they could be turned into a self-propelled model fish. This project shows how you can make a fun aquatic toy with household items in just minutes.

What's Needed

▶ Cardboard from a
  postcard or food
  container such as a
  cereal box

▶ Scissors

▶ Sink or bathtub filled with
  water

▶ Detergent

small
cardboard box

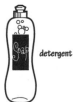
detergent

scissors

What to Do

Cut the shape of a fish from a piece of thin cardboard exactly as shown in **Figure 1**. Note the hole in the center and be sure to include the slit in the tail section.

FIGURE 1

Lay the cardboard fish on the surface of water. Then, carefully pour some detergent onto the circle on the fish. You'll soon see the little fish propel along like a motorboat. See **Figure 2**.

The detergent breaks up the water molecules, which are held together very tightly. As the water loses cohesiveness, it propels the fish model forward, as shown in **Figure 3**.

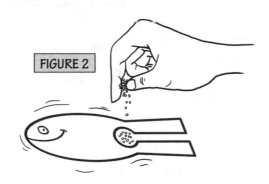

FIGURE 2

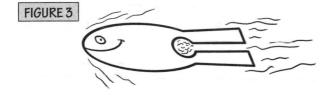

FIGURE 3

Jumping Tadpole

Origami models are fun to make. But the ones that give us added pleasure are animated figures.

With just a few paper folds, you can make a cute tadpole model that jumps up in the air when you press down on it.

What's Needed
▶ Paper
▶ Scissors
▶ Pencil or pen

scissors

paper

pencil

What to Do
Cut out a 4-inch square piece of paper, as shown in **Figure 1**. Fold the paper in half from the top and side and then unfold it. See **Figure 2**. Fold the corner sections toward the center. See **Figure 3**. Then, fold the left and right sides to the center, as shown in **Figure 4**.

Next, fold the bottom third section up and crease it. See **Figure 5**. Fold the bottom left and right corner sections toward the center, as shown in **Figure 6**.

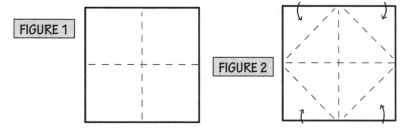

FIGURE 1

FIGURE 2

Last, fold the bottom section down, as shown in **Figure 7**. You can then use a pencil to draw eyes on the sneaky tadpole figure.

To make the tadpole jump, simply push down on its back, slide your finger back, and watch the little baby frog leap in the air, as shown in **Figure 8**.

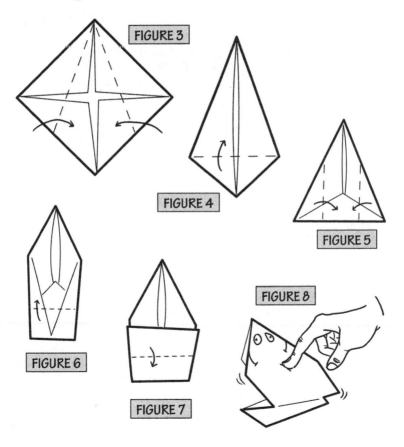

FIGURE 3

FIGURE 4

FIGURE 5

FIGURE 6

FIGURE 7

FIGURE 8

Science and Technology Resources

If you find that you like science and invention and want to go further in your quest for knowledge, this section provides a multitude of science education resources. You'll find links science fairs, science camps and schools, science organizations, and educational scholarships.

You'll also find special inventor resources and contests, grants and awards, free government programs, educator lesson plans, and additional links to free science project Web sites.

Science Freebies, Grants, and Scholarships
www.cos.com
www.science.doe.gov/grants
www.sciencemaster.com
www.siemens-foundation.org
www.teacherhelp.org/freebies.htm
www.thehomeschoolmom.com/teacherslounge/freebies.php

Inventors and Inventing
www.funology.com
www.inventivekids.com
http://inventors.about.com/od/campinventio1/index_r.htm
http://inventorsdigest.com
www.inventorshq.com/just%20for%20kids.htm

Science Fairs

www.astc.org/sciencecenters/find_scicenter.htm
www.campresource.com
www.childrensmuseums.org/visit/reciprocal.htm
http://physics.usc.edu/ScienceFairs
www.super-science-fair-projects.com

Science Sites

build-it-yourself.com
kidsinvent.org
sciencetoymaker.org
theteachersguide.com/QuickScienceActivities.html
wildplanet.com

Gadgets Sites

gizmodo.com
johnson-smith.com
popgadget.net
scientificsonline.com
smartplanet.net
thinkgeek.com

Survival Sites

simply-survival.com
skillsofsurvival.com
Survival.com
Survivalx.com

Science and Technology Sites

about.com
discover.com
howstuffworks.com
midnightscience.com
scienceproject.com
Scientificsonline.com
scitoys.com

Girls' Interest Sites

girlstech.douglass.rutgers.edu www.braincake.org
jfg.girlscouts.org
www.computergirl.us
www.gemsclub.org/index.html
www.girlscando.com/index.html
www.girlzone.com
www.sallyridescience.com/index.shtml
www.smartgirl.org

Other Web Sites Of Interest

Popsci.com
Popularmechanics.com
rube-goldberg.com
wildplanet.com

Recommended Books

Gonzo Gizmos (Simon Field, Chicago Review Press)

Joey Green's Encyclopedia of Offbeat Uses For Brand-Name Products
    (Joey Green, Prentice Hall)

*They All Laughed...From Light Bulbs to Lasers: The Fascinating Stories
    Behind the Great Inventions That Have Changed Our Lives* (Ira
    Flatow, Perennial)

Women Invent (Susan Casey, Wiley)

The Worst-Case Scenario Survival (Joshua Piven and David
    Borgenicht, Chronicle Books)

Recommended Magazines

Craft
Girl's Life
Make
Nuts and Volts
Popular Mechanics
Popular Science